Heritage Trees of Scotland

Rodger, Stokes & Ogilvie

Bowhill, Selkirk, Scotland

Foreword

by The Duke of Buccleuch, KT

The life-enhancing virtue of trees is beyond measure, but because their life span can be many times that of man's, we tend to regard them as permanent features to be taken for granted. However, if we just try to imagine the towns and cities without their parks, squares and tree-lined streets, or our rural landscape devoid of their most significant features, our appreciation of them is immediately sharpened. No matter whether they appear singly as humble hedgerow trees or avenues, in clumps and spinneys, as shelterbelts or in great forests, they are there to refresh the soul of man and physically purify the air we breathe.

Heritage Trees of Scotland comes at a time when 'short-termism' is taking over the long-term planning of our forebears, as exemplified by this selection of venerable trees. So much of our wonderful landscape and all within it, which we so greatly value today, is the direct result of the forethought of those living three or four hundred years ago. What an example this is for us to plan for future generations! Even the Fortingall Yew Tree in Perthshire, still living and probably 3000 years old at the time of the first Christmas, might be credited to one of our ancestors.

Introduction

Scotland is blessed with a rich and diverse legacy of "heritage" trees. Many are notable for their historical, cultural and botanical significance; some are extremely old; others have interesting historical associations; and most are full of character and impressive beauty. Other heritage trees are champions of record dimensions, boasting the tallest, largest-girthed and oldest trees in the United Kingdom, and there are others that carry the mantle by virtue of their special resonance in communities or because they are well-known landmarks. Many of these arboricultural treasures are the living legacy of Scotland's great tradition of tree collectors, planters, foresters and arboriculturalists. They stand as milestones of our cultural and natural heritage, a rich legacy for future generations to admire and enjoy.

Heritage Trees of Scotland grew out of Treefest Scotland 2002, a year-long programme of events co-ordinated by the Forestry Commission Scotland to celebrate Scotland's wonderful trees, woods and forests. As a contribution to Treefest, the Forestry Commission Scotland commissioned the compilation of an inventory of the country's most exceptional trees. The goal was to turn the spotlight on to an important part of our heritage to help ensure that special trees are not lost through ignorance of their worth. Some trees are as important to our heritage as the great stately homes, yet many are undervalued and little known.

The inventory was first presented to the public during 2002 as an Internet promotion on the Treefest website, www.treefestscotland.org.uk/heritage. A small panel of judges then faced the difficult task of selecting 100 of those trees to which they could award the accolade of "Heritage Tree of Scotland". These were to include the most important specimens, such as those of European and even global significance. The authors and the judging panel stress, though, that the 100 trees presented in this book are just some of the most wonderful specimens that grace Scotland's urban and rural landscapes – the list is by no means exhaustive, and there is little doubt that many more exceptional trees remain to be discovered and recorded.

This book describes each of the 100 trees selected and explains why they were chosen. Many have their own stories to tell, perhaps through their role in history or legend. Some have been used as special meeting places, or as the sites of trials and executions, and others have associations with royalty – although it is often difficult to tell where history ends and legend begins.

In some cases age plays an important part. We know, for example, that oaks can live for centuries. Some are as old as our medieval cathedrals and are equally worthy of protection. But it is the yews that really stretch the imagination, because they can live for thousands of years. Indeed, the oldest tree in Britain, the Fortingall Yew, could be as much as 5,000 years old – as old as Stonehenge!

The chosen trees also include examples of exceptional rarity, beauty or national interest. Nor are they all native to this land, because some belong to species that have been introduced from far-flung parts of the world and are now flourishing in Scotland's cool, damp climate. Indeed, one or two are the very first individuals of their species introduced to Scotland.

Through the support of the Forestry Commission Scotland, the owners and custodians of these trees have been presented with certificates and specially commissioned wooden sculptures in recognition of the status and importance of their trees. Many of these splendid trees are accessible to the public, (but readers are reminded to seek the owners' permission before visiting trees on private agricultural land, estates and gardens).

We hope this book will add to readers' interest and enjoyment should they decide to visit some of these amazing trees. If they do, they are reminded of that important environmental principle, "Leave nothing but footprints, take nothing but photographs". That way, generations to come will be able to share our admiration for these wonderful trees.

Finally, readers are invited to notify the authors of any other exceptional trees they might know about in Scotland that are not recorded in this book or on the website. They should write, giving reasons why the trees are special and a precise location (an Ordnance Survey reference is best) to:

Heritage Trees of Scotland,
c/o James Ogilvie,
Forestry Commission Scotland,
231 Corstorphine Road,
Edinburgh,
EH12 7AT.

E-mail: james.ogilvie@forestry.gsi.gov.uk

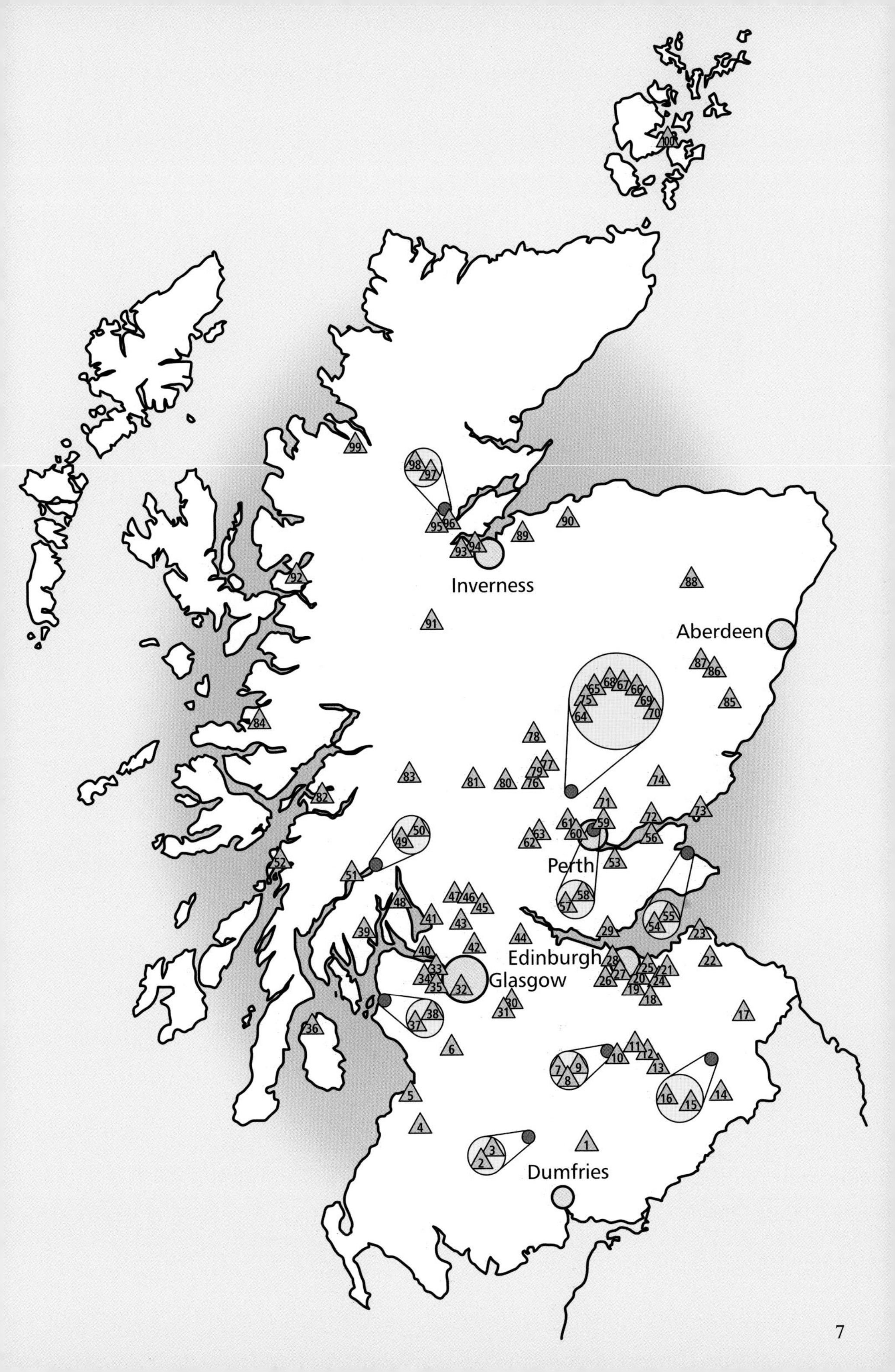
Inverness
Aberdeen
Perth
Edinburgh
Glasgow
Dumfries

The Lochwood Oaks

A small stand of ancient sessile oaks *(Quercus petraea)* lies close to Lochwood Tower, near Moffat, Dumfries and Galloway. These trees are the surviving remnants of a long-established oak forest dating back many centuries, and include individuals of great age and character. This valuable population of veteran trees now supports an important range of wildlife and lichens.

During the 1970s, the trees at Lochwood played an important role in the development of dendrochronology: the study of annual rings to date wooden artefacts and past events. As a tree grows, it puts on an annual growth ring. Because trees grow at different rates according to the weather, they have wider rings in favourable years and narrower rings in unfavourable years. Sequences of tree-rings thus give unique patterns which reflect changes in climate over a long period of time. The ring sequence, taken as a core sample, also provides a unique 'fingerprint' which can be detected in other trees growing in the same geographical area.

The old oaks at Lochwood allowed scientists to construct a ring sequence from 1571 to 1970. Once this tree ring sequence had been established, timbers in local buildings could be compared to the sequence, providing accurate dates for when the building was constructed. This technique has proved so useful that many universities and laboratories around the world are currently establishing their own tree ring sequences to aid in the dating of wood.

Location: Lochwood Castle, near Moffat, Dumfries and Galloway.
The site is an SSSI and public access is limited.

The Drumlanrig Sycamore

Location: Parkland close to Drumlanrig Castle and its main access drive, off the A76 road about 4.8 kilometres (3 miles) north of Thornhill, Dumfries and Galloway. The grounds are open to the public and admission charges apply.

An imposing sycamore *(Acer pseudoplatanus)* grows in the parkland of Drumlanrig Castle, near Thornhill, Dumfriesshire. At least 300 years old, it has reached an immense size and has a perfect, dome-like canopy. The trunk measures 7.06 metres (23 feet) in girth and the lofty crown has attained 31.5 metres (103 feet) in height. This single tree contains 25 cubic metres (883 cubic feet) of timber and the canopy covers 800 square metres (8611 square feet).

Sycamore, also known in Scotland as 'plane' or 'plain', was a popular species by the mid-seventeenth century. The 6th Earl of Haddington wrote in 1761 that "there is no old seat, no gentleman's house, nor any place where old trees are, but the plains are the most numerious". [1]

The Drumlanrig Douglas

One of David Douglas's (see page 96) original introductions of Douglas fir *(Pseudotsuga menziesii)* to the United Kingdom survives in the extensive grounds of the Duke of Buccleuch's Drumlanrig estate, near Thornhill, Dumfries and Galloway. This was grown from the first seed brought into Scotland in 1827. Douglas's brother, John, was Clerk of Works at Drumlanrig, hence the connection. The tree is a fine specimen, with a single, straight trunk measuring 5.18 metres (17 feet) in girth and reaching 42.0 metres (138 feet) in height.

Location: A small area of woodland to the north of Drumlanrig Castle, off the A76 road about 4.8 kilometres (3 miles) north of Thornhill, Dumfries and Galloway. The grounds are open to the public, and admission charges apply.

SYCAMORE

Blairquhan Dool Tree

A 'dool' or 'dule' tree was once used as a natural gallows for hanging criminals. They were common features on many estates until the middle of the eighteenth century. Such trees normally occupied a prominent location near the laird's residence, where the corpse was left to swing as a deterrent for all to see. The favoured species used for this purpose was sycamore, because its strong and resilient timber was unlikely to fail at the crucial moment. The name 'dool' derives from old Scots and means sorrowful or mournful.

One of Scotland's few surviving dool trees is the ancient sycamore *(Acer pseudoplatanus)* that stands in the shadow of Blairquhan Castle, near Straiton, Ayrshire. The tree is thought to have been planted about 1500 during the reign of James V of Scotland. The moss-covered trunk has a girth of 5.59 metres (18 feet 4 inches) and is completely hollow, with only a very thin outer shell of sound wood supporting the tree. The once spreading crown was heavily pruned in 1997 in an effort to preserve the fragile shell and prevent the much-weakened trunk from total collapse. Vigorous new growth is now establishing a new, smaller crown. This unwitting instrument of execution will remain in the land of the living for a while yet.

Location: Close to Blairquhan House, Blairquhan estate, off the B741 road about 1.6 kilometres (1 mile) west of Straiton, South Ayrshire. The house and grounds are open to the public during the last two weeks of July and the first two weeks of August, or by appointment. Admission charges apply.

Rabbie Burns' Sycamore

The fine, large sycamore *(Acer pseudoplatanus)* that dominates Alloway Auld Kirk, built in 1516, has taken the name of the National Bard. Robert Burns (1759 – 1796), who was born a stone's throw from the kirk, was inspired by this eerie setting and later immortalised the kirk in his famous work, 'Tam O' Shanter':

> 'When, glimmering through the groaning trees,
> Kirk-Alloway seem'd in a bleeze,
> Through ilka bore the beams were glancing,
> And loud resounding mirth and dancing.'

The grand and imposing sycamore, which appears to emerge from the foundations of the ancient kirk, certainly adds to the atmosphere. The shapely, spreading crown is 22.5 metres (74 feet) tall and the single, squat trunk has a girth of 3.8 metres (12 feet 6 inches). At some time in the past the church wall has been carefully bridged over the swollen root buttresses to accommodate its ever-increasing girth. Its date of origin and provenance is unknown, although judging by its dimensions, it probably began growing in the eighteenth century.

It is tempting to imagine that this gentle giant that now watches over 'Alloway's Auld Haunted Kirk' was around when the young Burns began writing poems inspired by the natural world around him.

Location: Next to the ruins of Alloway Auld Kirk, in the village of Alloway on the southern outskirts of Ayr, South Ayrshire. Free public access is available throughout the year.

The Auld Yew Tree of Loudoun

Location: On the south façade of the impressive ruin of Loudon Castle, off the A719 road about 1.6 kilometres (1 mile) north of Galston, East Ayrshire. It now forms the centrepiece of a theme park that is open to the public from April to October.

An ancient yew *(Taxus baccata)*, affectionately known as the 'Auld Yew Tree of Loudoun', stands in the shadow of the ruined walls of Loudon Castle, near Galston, East Ayrshire. It is said that one of the Loudoun family charters was signed under the yew in the time of William the Lion (1165 – 1214), and that the drafts of the Treaty of Union with England in 1603 were negotiated and discussed under its canopy. [1]

When Lord James of Loudon went into voluntary exile in Holland, he devised a cunning method of corresponding with his family back on his estate. For fear of detection, he addressed his letters to "The Gudewife of Auldton, at the Auld Yew Tree of Loudoun". Remarkably, they always reached their intended destination. [1]

The trunk of the yew measures 5.34 metres (17 feet 6 inches) in girth. When the original castle, dating from the fifteenth century, was heavily extended in 1811, the walls came within two metres of the trunk, and have left the crown very one-sided.

The tree is clearly a great survivor. In 1941, during World War II, while Belgian troops were stationed at the castle, it was accidentally gutted by fire and has remained a ruin ever since. How the yew survived the inferno is a mystery.

The Dawyck Silver Fir

Location: Dawyck Botanic Garden, off the B712 road about 11.3 kilometres (7 miles) south west of Peebles, Scottish Borders. Public access is available mid February until mid November. The garden is one of the regional gardens of the National Botanical Gardens of Scotland.

The European silver fir *(Abies alba)* with the earliest known planting date in Scotland stands in Dawyck Botanic Garden, near Peebles. This was reputed to have been planted in 1680 by the Veitch family. Despite the crown now looking rather tattered and straggly, this is still a fine example of Europe's principal fir. Its trunk measures 5.4 metres (17 feet 9 inches) in girth and its height is recorded as 35 metres (115 feet).

The silver fir was introduced to the United Kingdom from central Europe in 1603 (see page 80). The species grows well in Scotland and it was widely planted during the eighteenth and nineteenth centuries.

The Dawyck Larch

Location:
See page 18

One of the few surviving European larches *(Larix decidua)* introduced to Scotland in 1725 by Sir James Naesmyth stands in the Dawyck Botanic Garden, near Peebles. This is one of the earliest surviving plantings in Scotland of a species that was ultimately to have a major impact on commercial forestry practice (see The Kailzie Larch, page 22). Now measuring 4.46 metres (14 feet 7 inches) in girth and 33 metres (108 feet) tall, it is still a fine tree.

Sir James Naesmyth (1644 – 1754) was a renowned collector of trees from around the world and his early plantings were to establish the fine collection that forms Dawyck Botanic Garden.

The Dawyck Beech

Location:
See page 18

The 'Dawyck Beech' (*Fagus sylvatica* 'Dawyck') takes its name from the Peeblesshire estate where it was first discovered. While planting a beech wood in 1860, a sharp-eyed forester noticed a single sapling with an unusual form, its branches sweeping tightly upwards. The laird, Sir John Murray Naesmyth (1803 – 1876), had it replanted in the policy woodlands near Dawyck House. When the estate changed hands in 1897, it was the new owner, F R S Balfour, who brought this natural mutant to popular attention, so that by 1912 it was officially referred to as 'Dawyck beech'. The original tree still stands in good health and has retained its upright form and spire-like crown.

The Posso Sycamores

The Posso sycamores *(Acer pseudoplantanus)* are a pair of magnificent trees standing in a remote Peeblesshire glen close to the ruins of sixteenth-century Posso Tower.

One specimen close to the tower boasts the title of the largest-girthed sycamore recorded in the United Kingdom, its trunk measuring an astonishing 8.54 metres (28 feet). Large buttress roots sprawl over the uneven ground and between the scattered masonry of the tower.

Its partner stands isolated in the middle of a grazed field, with a perfectly symmetrical crown. Although its girth is smaller, it is still an impressive 7.06 metres (23 feet) and reaches a height of 27.5 metres (90 feet).

Location: Privately owned farmland about 200 metres west of Posso Farm farmhouse. The farm is about eight kilometres (5 miles) along an unclassifed road that runs south towards Kirkton Manor and Posso from a junction with the A72 about 2.4 kilometres (1.5 miles) west of Peebles. Access is available only with permission.

The Kailzie Larch

The oldest surviving European larches *(Larix decidua)* in Scotland date from 1725, when some of the trees were introduced to a few Peeblesshire estates by Sir James Naesmyth (1644 – 1754), Laird of Posso and Dawyck.

One of the finest specimens can be found at Kailzie Gardens, near Peebles. The larch's introduction to the estate is amusingly recounted by a member of the Innerleithen Alpine Club following a visit to the estate in 1890:

'In 1725, on returning from London, Sir James brought with him in his carriage some young larches, and he called in passing and dined with his friend the Laird of Kailzie. This Laird of Posso and Dawyck, like his father 'The Deil', had trees on the brain and no doubt over the wine waxed eloquent about the new importation. The result was that one specimen was planted next morning in Kailzie Park, and is still standing there, growing vigorously and without symptom of decay. Its height is 105 feet and its circumference four feet from the ground is twelve feet.' [1]

The straight, unblemished trunk now measures 4.8 metres (15 feet 9 inches) girth at 1.22 metres (4 feet) above the ground, a respectable increase of 1.13 metres (3 feet 9 inches) since 1890. It supports a crown that has developed huge, up-curved limbs typically seen in many old larches.

Location: Kailzie Garden, off the B7062 road about 4.8 kilometres (3 miles) south east of Peebles, Scottish Borders. The garden is open to the public seven days a week throughout the year.

Traquair House Yews

Location: On the edge of woodland and next to a footpath along the banks of the Quair Water, east of Traquair House, off the B709 road and about 1.6 kilometres (1 mile) south of Innerleithen, Scottish Borders. Traquair House is open to the public from mid April to the end of October.

Four ancient yew trees *(Taxus baccata)* stand in the grounds of historic Traquair House, near the Border town of Innerleithen. Dating from the early twelfth century, Traquair House is reputedly the oldest continuously inhabited dwelling in Scotland. It has been visited by many of Scotland's prominent historical figures, including Mary, Queen of Scots and Bonnie Prince Charlie.

Forming a close group near the banks of the Quair Water, the four yews are of outlandish shape and form. Their hunched and twisted limbs give the impression of four old men bent over in discussion, and the dark inner cavern formed by their dense foliage is eerily atmospheric.

The Tinnis Ash

What is probably Scotland's oldest ash tree *(Fraxinus excelsior)* forms part of an important remnant of wood pasture in Bowhill estate. The partially collapsed remains of this once exceptionally large specimen are still very much alive, and this ancient veteran continues to thrive in its rural setting. The trunk might have originally measured between 9 and 10 metres (33 feet) in girth before it became so rotten that it eventually collapsed and part was lost. The remaining fragments present an intriguing framework of sculptural beauty. Ash as a species is not known for its longevity or great size. However, in exceptional circumstances it is clearly capable of both.

Location: A grazed field about 30 metres south of the A708 road, eight kilometres (5 miles) west of Selkirk, Scottish Borders. Access is available only with permission.

The Capon Tree

The Capon Tree, a hollow English oak *(Quercus robur)*, is one of the last survivors of the ancient Jed Forest. About 1000 years old, this celebrated tree has been a constant feature in the turbulent history of the border country. The origin of the tree's name is uncertain, but it could have been derived from the word 'capuche', the hood worn by the monks who sheltered under its branches on their way to the nearby Jedburgh Abbey.

According to tradition, border clans rallied for action at the tree during the troubled days of the sixteenth century. Living in a border town, Jedburgh's local families were involved in fighting the English, and the Jethart Callants had a reputation for outstanding bravery. Both they and the Capon Tree are celebrated annually at the Jedburgh Callants' Festival. Each July 'The Callant' – a young man chosen to represent the town - leads his mounted cavalcade on historic rides, the most important being to Redeswire to commemorate the last cross-border skirmish. On Festival Day, the Callant visits Ferniehurst Castle and on his return home stops at the Capon Tree, taking a sprig and wearing it in the lapel of his jacket.

Edwardian postcard of the tree, viewed from the other side.

Location: On the banks of the River Jed and alongside the A68 less than 3 kilometres (2 miles) south of Jedburgh town centre, accessible by a 15-minute walk from the town on pavements all the way, starting from the first bridge (near the Abbey). The tree is around the corner on the right just after the third bridge.

St Boswells Apple

This solitary crab apple *(Malus sylvestris)* is a Scottish champion in terms of its girth. Standing in a field near the Scottish Borders town of St Boswells, the substantial trunk measures 2.41 metres (8 feet) in girth and the crown reaches 10.2 metres (34 feet) in height. This is a fine old example of our native species of apple.

Location: A field close to Fens Farm, St Boswells, Scottish Borders. A public footpath passes close by the tree.

The Dryburgh Abbey Yew

Within the tranquil ruins of Dryburgh Abbey, near the Borders town of St Boswells, stands an ancient yew *(Taxus baccata)* alleged to have been planted by monks in 1136. The planting of yew trees at places of religious worship was common practice at that time.

The yew is an unassuming specimen of no great size, with a trunk girth of 3.86 metres (12 feet 8 inches). Historical growth measurements indicate a very slow rate of growth, which suggests that it might indeed have originated in the early twelfth century, thus predating the foundation of the abbey by Hugh de Moreville in 1150.

Location: The private grounds of Dryburgh Abbey House, St Boswells, Scottish Borders. It can easily be viewed from the adjacent grounds of the Abbey, which are in the care of Historic Scotland and to which public access is available all year.

The Polwarth Thorn

Location: Enclosed by iron railings at the site of the old Polwarth village, off the A6112 road about 6.4 kilometres (4 miles) south of Duns, Scottish Borders. Public access is available.

The Scottish Borders village of Polwarth was abandoned many years ago and little evidence remains of its existence. However, the famous Polwarth hawthorn *(Crataegus monogyna)*, which once stood in pride of place on the village green, still survives. Newly married couples used to dance around the ancient thorn tree, a local custom and tradition that continued for centuries. Indeed, the tree was immortalised by the poet Allan Ramsay (1686 – 1758) in his poem 'Polwarth, On The Green':

'At Polwarth on the Green,
If you'll meet me in the morn,
Where lads and lasses do convene
To dance around the thorn.'

The original hawthorn tree has died, but has been replaced by its own saplings over the years. Two thorn trees, enclosed by iron railings, still occupy the site.

Hawthorn is strongly associated with pagan Mayday rites, and the blossoms of 'the May' are said to symbolise love, betrothal and fertility. It is a species that is steeped in folklore and mythology and was revered as a sacred tree in Celtic Scotland.

Location: Private parkland close to Prestonhall House, near Pathhead, Midlothian. Public access is available at certain times throughout the year, or with permission of the owner.

The Prestonhall Beech

One of the largest known beech trees *(Fagus sylvatica)* in Scotland is the fine, open-grown specimen that stands in the parkland close to Prestonhall House, near Pathhead, Midlothian. The tree is more than 30 metres (98 feet) tall and its immense trunk measures 6.69 metres (22 feet) in girth. This tree is a first-class example of a species that was planted on many country estates, and which grows particularly well in the fertile lands of Lothian.

Beech as a species is not renowned for its longevity and few trees exceed 250 years old before decay takes its toll.

The Roslin Sweet Chestnut

An ancient sweet chestnut *(Castanea sativa)* stands in woodland near the mysterious Rosslyn Chapel. Its vast and heavily burred trunk has an impressive girth of 7.72 metres (25 feet 4 inches), one of the largest in Scotland. The crown consists of a contorted framework of large, skeletal limbs, and only the occasional sprig of live foliage and vigorous basal shoots continue to keep this time-weary veteran alive.

The chestnut is probably between 400 and 450 years old. It stands next to the moss-covered ruins of Rosebank House, once the residence of the Dowager Countess of Rosslyn. The house is also noteworthy as the birthplace of the poet, author and songwriter Hector McNeill (1746 - 1818).

Location: Woodland on the south bank of Roslin Glen, about 300 metres east of Rosslyn Chapel, south of Roslin, Midlothian. The footpath passes close to the tree and there is free public access.

Rizzio's Chestnut

Melville Castle was frequented by Mary, Queen of Scots. During one of her visits, David Rizzio, her Italian secretary and close companion, is said to have planted a tree as a token of his love for her by the banks of the River North Esk. The tree, an ancient sweet chestnut *(Castanea sativa)*, survives to this day next to the stable block, now known appropriately as 'Chestnut House'.

However, such blatant displays of love were to be Rizzio's downfall. He was murdered before the Queen's eyes in the Palace of Holyrood House in 1566 by a group of conspirators led by Mary's jealous second husband, Lord Darnley. Rizzio's chestnut remains today as an enduring symbol of his ill-fated affection for Mary.

The tree is a fine old specimen of huge girth, and it is quite feasible that it did indeed originate in the mid-1560s. The vast trunk is 7.63 metres (25 feet) in girth. Like all ancient sweet chestnuts, it is of no significant height and has died back to 16.7 metres (55 feet). The crown is of reasonable shape, although abundant deadwood indicates that it is in the natural process of decline. However, the capacity for the species to regenerate itself by forming a new crown from dormant buds should guarantee its presence for a few more centuries at least.

Location: The private garden of Chestnut House, about 100 metres south west of Melville Castle, near Dalkeith, Midlothian. Access is available only with written permission.

The Great Yew of Ormiston

Early woodcut of John Knox, from Beza's *Icones* (1580)

This is a first-class example of the few 'layering' yews *(Taxus baccata)* known in Scotland. Weeping branches radiate out from the solid central trunk and take root where they touch the ground, encircling the tree in an ever-extending fringe of growth. The inner 'chamber' formed by the layered branches and dense foliage creates a spacious, natural cathedral of arching limbs. The huge central trunk measures 6.94 metres (22 feet 10 inches) in girth. Records of measurement over the past 160 years suggest a very slow rate of increment, and it is perfectly feasible that the tree could be as old as 1000 years.

As early as the fifteenth century the yew was recognised as a local landmark: a parchment dated 1474, found among some old papers belonging to the Earl of Hopetoun, had been signed under the yew tree. [1]

The famous religious reformer, John Knox (c. 1514 – 1572), who was born in nearby Haddington, is also reputed to have preached his early sermons within the secluded interior of the yew's evergreen canopy. Here Knox, along with his influential mentor, George Wishart, sowed the seeds of the Reformation which was ultimately to sweep throughout Scotland.

Location: A private residential development close to the ruins of Ormiston Hall, Ormiston, East Lothian. It is reached from the A6093.

The Whittinghame Yew

One of Scotland's most famous and remarkable yew trees *(Taxus baccata)* stands in the East Lothian estate of Whittinghame.

Legend has it that in 1566 a dark deed was plotted in the sepulchral shade of this ancient yew – the murder of Mary, Queen of Scots' second husband, Lord Darnley. The conspirators included Lord Morton, resident in nearby Whittinghame Castle, and the Earl of Bothwell, Mary's lover and third husband-to-be. Darnley met his untimely end in 1567 when his Edinburgh lodgings were blown up.[1] The yew remains forever linked with this event in Scottish history.

This tree is one of Scotland's 'layering' yews, its ever-increasing ring of outer growth covering a vast area of ground, radiating with perfect symmetry from a single, central trunk. The dense canopy of graceful branches and dark foliage sweep to the ground, where they take root and layer. This forms a spacious inner sanctum that can only be accessed by a low entry tunnel through the outer ring of foliage.

The relatively small trunk, measuring 3.64 metres (12 feet) in girth, belies the tree's great age. Historical measurements indicate a very slow rate of growth, with an increase of only 0.4 metres (1 foot 4 inches) in girth over the past 110 years, so this yew might well be as much as 1000 years old.

Location: Near Whittinghame Tower, near East Linton, East Lothian. Access is available only by prior permission.

Location: The eastern slopes of North Berwick Law, immediately south of North Berwick, East Lothian. Sign-posted public car parking is available and well defined footpaths lead to the trees. Free public access is available all year.

Act of Union Beeches

Clinging to the windswept slopes of North Berwick Law is a gaunt group of beech trees *(Fagus sylvatica)*, planted to commemorate the Act of Union between the Scottish and English Parliaments in 1707. The local laird, Sir Hew Dalrymple, was one of the signatories to the Act.

The original planting comprised a small woodland, but all that remains is a group of eight bedraggled trees. Given their harsh growing environment, the trees have attained a respectable size, the tallest standing 31.2 metres (102 feet) high and the largest girth measuring 3.23 metres (10 feet 7 inches). Their thin, smooth bark has been wind-blasted to a silvery whiteness.

The Newbattle Abbey Sycamore

This fine sycamore *(Acer pseudoplatanus)* growing in the grounds of Newbattle Abbey, on the outskirts of Dalkeith, is reputedly the oldest example of the species in Scotland, and perhaps in the UK; it is thought to have been planted around 1550. Despite its great age, it is still an imposing tree, dominating the frontage of the house. The height of the crown, which is now very stag-headed, measures 26 metres (85 feet) and the trunk has a girth of 5.5 metres (18 feet). Many of the big old sycamores in Scotland, originally known as 'plane', were probably brought here from France during the time of the Reformation in the mid-sixteenth century. [1]

Location: To the front of Newbattle Abbey, Dalkeith, Midlothian. The abbey now functions as a private adult residential college. Access with permission only.

Dalkeith Park Oaks

A large group of veteran oak trees grows in the grounds of Dalkeith Palace; formerly a deer-park. According to annual ring counts, most of the trees date from between 1580 and 1617, though some of them may have been planted as early as the fourteenth century. They display huge multi-stemmed trunks, indicating that they have been coppiced early in their lives. The largest bases reach almost 10 metres (33 feet) in girth. [1]

This collection of oaks presents a rare landscape feature, a habitat of national importance, and a home to many endangered invertebrate species. Veteran trees are vital elements of woodland ecosystems and have tremendous nature conservation value.

Location: Parkland north of Dalkeith Palace, Midlothian. The estate is owned by the Duke of Buccleuch and the grounds are managed as a country park. Public access is available.

The Four Disciples

Huddled together in Malleny Garden, on the outskirts of Edinburgh, stand four clipped yews *(Taxus baccata)* affectionately known as the 'Four Disciples'. They are the sole survivors of a group of 12 trees, said to represent Christ's disciples. Unfortunately, eight were felled by a previous owner of the property as recently as 1961, which serves to highlight the ever-present threat to many of our important heritage trees. The garden and its remaining 'disciples' are now in the care of the National Trust for Scotland. Nearby Malleny House was built for Sir James Murray in 1635 and the 12 Disciples were probably planted about that time.

Location: The walled garden at Malleny Garden, sign-posted on the eastern edge of the Edinburgh suburb of Balerno. Malleny Garden is owned by the National Trust for Scotland and is open to the public.

R L Stevenson aged 39

Stevenson's Yew

The famous Scottish author, Robert Louis Stevenson (1850 – 1894), spent part of his childhood with his maternal grandfather at Colinton Manse, Edinburgh. He is known to have played in the spreading branches of the old yew tree *(Taxus baccata)* in the garden. The remains of his swing are still evident on one of the limbs. Stevenson fondly recalls his early days at the manse in the company of the ancient tree:

> 'A yew, which is one of the glories of the village. Under the circuit of its wide, black branches, it was always dark and cool, and there was a green scurf over all the trunk among which glistened the round, bright drops of resin.' [1]

The tree also provided inspiration for his poetry:

> 'Below the yew – it still is there –
> Our phantom voices haunt the air
> As we were still at play,
> And I can hear them call and say,
> '*How far is it to Babylon?*' [2]

The tree is thought to be several centuries old and is recorded in the Kirk Session minutes of 1630. It is a fine specimen, with the trunk measuring 3.64 metres (12 feet) in girth. Despite losing some of its lower branches, the yew still stands today, a living link with one of Scotland's great literary figures.

Location: The private garden of Colinton Manse, Dell Road, Edinburgh.

This fine example of Corstorphine sycamore reflects the original splendour of the Mother tree.

Location: A private garden on Dovecot Road, near its junction with Saughton Road North, in Corstorphine, a suburb of Edinburgh. Access is available only with permission.

The Corstorphine Sycamore

For centuries, the Corstorphine sycamore was one of Edinburgh's finest living landmarks. Its bright yellow foliage, which flushes several weeks earlier than is normal for the species, marks it out as unusual. It has been recognised as a distinct botanical variety and named *Acer pseudoplatanus* 'Corstorphinense', or Corstorphine sycamore, in recognition of its origin in the Edinburgh suburb.

The sycamore is thought to have been planted about 1600, and is steeped in local history and tradition. Despite being reduced to a shattered stump in the Boxing Day gale of 1998, the original tree continues to survive by producing vigorous new shoots.

The Cockairnie Sweet Chestnut

The sweet chestnut *(Castanea sativa)* at Cockairnie House, near Aberdour, Fife, holds the honour of being the largest-girthed example of its species in Scotland. It has a remarkable girth of 8.82 metres (29 feet), and it would take six fully grown adults with outstretched arms linked together to encircle the trunk. Cockairnie House is about 500 years old and the tree was probably planted shortly after the house was built.

Wider than it is tall, the tree has a vast, pot-bellied trunk that appears to consist of one huge burr around its entire circumference. This natural growth deformity undoubtedly exaggerates its great girth.

Location: The private garden of Cockcairnie House, about 3.2 kilometres (2 miles) west of Aberdour, Fife. Access is available only with permission.

The Covenanters' Oak

The lone veteran known as the 'Covenanters' Oak' stands just off the main avenue to historic Dalzell House, on the outskirts of Motherwell, North Lanarkshire. It takes its name from the movement of Scottish Presbyterians who, in 1638, covenanted to defend their church from the influence of Charles I and his attempt to introduce the English Prayer Book. The Hamilton family, who held Dalzell Estate at the time, were sympathetic to the Covenanters' cause and provided protection to its more troublesome ringleaders. One such notable character was the Reverend John Lauder, who is said to have preached to 400 Covenanters under the boughs of the great oak, which provided a natural gathering point for the clandestine religious meetings.

The huge English, or pedunculate oak *(Quercus robur)* is thought to be an isolated survivor of an extensive deer park and hunting estate planted by King David I in the mid-twelfth century, which would make it a contemporary of the veterans just across the River Clyde at Cadzow (see page 50). The imposing trunk now measures an impressive 6.69 metres (22 feet) in girth. The fine old oak stands to this day in good health, a living reminder of a tumultuous period in Scotland's religious history.

Location: Next to the main driveway about 400 metres west of Dalzell House in Dalzell Estate Country Park, off Dalzell Drive on the southern outskirts of Motherwell, North Lanarkshire. The country park is managed by North Lanarkshire Council and free public access is available throughout the year.

The Cadzow Oaks

This internationally important group of about 300 sessile oaks *(Quercus petraea)* includes some of the oldest and largest examples of the species in Scotland. They are thought to have been planted by King David I (1124 - 1153) in the mid-twelfth century, when he used nearby Cadzow Castle as a hunting base. If, indeed, they are contemporary with David I, they rank among the oldest broadleaved trees in Scotland. The surviving collection of veteran trees now represents a rare example of medieval wood pasture. Most of the oaks fall within a Site of Special Scientific Interest because of the unique habitat they provide for rare and endangered insects.

The individual trees are particularly notable for their contorted trunks, which are heavily burred and have great girths. Having grown in an open situation and been subject to centuries of under-grazing, they have assumed a variety of unusual shapes. Each is a living sculpture with a unique signature of swellings, twists, ridges and cavities. Many trees are noticeably stag-headed, with an array of dead, sun-bleached branches protruding from the live crowns. This is a typical characteristic of veteran trees and part of their natural survival mechanism. As trees age and their trunks start to deteriorate, they conserve resources by dying back and forming new, more compact crowns.

Location: Access to most of these trees is restricted, but three fine specimens stand in neighbouring Chatelherault Country Park and are accessible to the public. Chatelherault Country Park is on the south east outskirts of Hamilton, South Lanarkshire, and is well sign-posted off the A72 road. The oaks are sign-posted from the visitor centre. The Country Park is owned and managed by South Lanarkshire Council and free public access is available throughout the year.

The Pollok Park Beech

The grossly distorted trunk of this beech *(Fagus sylvatica)* never ceases to amaze visitors. The trunk consists of a swollen and heavily gnarled mass of burrs and branches that appear to have amalgamated through time to form a huge, contorted ball extending from ground level up to 3 metres (9 feet 10 inches). From this massive structure a number of relatively small limbs radiate in all directions to form a low, spreading crown. The trunk is of huge proportions, measuring 7 metres (23 feet) in girth at ground level and expanding to 10 metres (32 feet 10 inches) in girth at its widest point.

Thought to be about 250 years old, this eccentric of the arboricultural world has become a well known focal point in Glasgow's Pollok Park, where it stands atop a small podium in the gardens behind Pollok House. How this prominent tree assumed its outlandish shape is open to conjecture. Perhaps some genetic aberration, coupled with repeated pruning over a long period, might explain its strange form.

The lands of Pollok have been held by the Maxwell family for 700 years. Major plantings by the seventh baronet, Sir John Maxwell (1768 – 1844) and the tenth baronet, Sir John Stirling Maxwell (1866 – 1956), have created a wonderful treescape and lasting legacy for the people of Glasgow.

Location: The gardens behind Pollok House, Glasgow. Free public access is available throughout year.

The Dargarvel Hornbeam

A remarkable example of hornbeam *(Carpinus betulus)* is the vast, layering specimen that stands near Dargarvel House, at Bishopton, Renfrewshire. It is one of the largest and oldest known in Scotland and is thought to have been planted about the time of major remodelling work to Dargarvel House in 1670.

The low branches of this tree extend over a wide area, taking root and layering as they go. They form a contorted, sprawling mass covering an area of 1320 square metres (one third of an acre). The central hub of this extraordinary tree is a short, squat trunk measuring 4.11 metres (13 feet 6 inches) in girth.

Location: Dargarvel House, about 1.6 kilometres (1 mile) south of Bishopton, Renfrewshire. It forms part of a large ordnance factory and access is strictly controlled.

The Craigends Yew

The Craigends yew *(Taxus baccata)* is a sprawling monster of a tree. One of the biggest and oldest of its type in Scotland, the low, layering canopy spreads over the banks of the River Gryffe in Renfrewshire. Large branches descend to ground level, where they take root and proliferate in an impenetrable jungle of twisting branches. The circumference of the crown is quite remarkable, at 100 metres (328 feet), and the huge trunk measures 8.29 metres (27 feet 3 inches) in girth at ground level. The exact age and provenance of the Craigends Yew is unknown, although it is estimated to be between 500 and 700 years old.

Location: The banks of the River Gryffe in Houston, Renfrewshire, next to Yew Tree Gardens. A public footpath passes close to the tree, which is identified by an interpretation plaque. Free public access is available throughout the year.

The Wallace Yew

Location: A small public park in Elderslie, Renfrewshire, at the junction of Main Road and Wallace Avenue. Free public access is available throughout the year.

Detail of a sculpture of William Wallace, in the image of 'Braveheart' actor Mel Gibson.

Of all the trees associated with Scotland's popular hero, William Wallace (c1270 - 1305), it is the old yew *(Taxus baccata)* at Elderslie in Renfrewshire that is the most legitimate contender. Known locally as the 'Wallace Yew', it stands near the ruined house where Wallace was reputedly born.

Local legend has it that the tree was a sapling when Wallace was born and that he played in its branches as a child. However, although the tree is of considerable antiquity, it is unlikely to have existed in Wallace's day. A more plausible theory is that it was grown from a seed or shoot of an ancient yew that did stand in Wallace's time. With a girth of 4.3 metres (14 feet) and height of 12.0 metres (39 feet), the tree has been estimated to be between 350 and 400 years old.

Although sorely neglected in the past, it is slowly recovering from severe fire damage which all but killed it in 1978. This yew is a great survivor. Aided by a restoration programme implemented by Renfrewshire Council it is now putting on new growth. Like Wallace, this tree is a fighter, and will be around for a while yet.

The Arran Whitebeams

The Isle of Arran is home to two species of tree which do not occur anywhere else in the world, the Arran whitebeam *(Sorbus arranensis)* and the Arran cut-leaved whitebeam *(Sorbus pseudofennica)*. They are also Scotland's rarest native trees, and in global terms are officially classed as dangerously close to extinction by the WWF.

Only a few hundred trees of each species exist, clinging perilously to the steep rocky slopes of two remote glens at the north of the island. The Arran whitebeam was first recorded in 1897 and is thought to have arisen as a natural hybrid between the rock whitebeam *(Sorbus rupicola)* and the ubiquitous rowan *(Sorbus aucuparia)*. The other rare hybrid, the Arran cut-leaved whitebeam, was first noted in 1952. This appears to have arisen from the Arran whitebeam back-crossing with the rowan. Both species were more abundant in the past, but have been forced to retreat to their restricted enclaves as the island was progressively improved for agriculture.

Sorbus pseudofennica.

Location: Glens Catacol and Diomhan, approximately 3.2 kilometres (2 miles) south west of Lochranza, Isle of Arran.

Small, windswept and stunted, these uniquely Scottish trees are under constant threat from the strong gales and heavy snow storms common in their montane habitat, because the fragile root systems are easily dislodged from the rocky soil.

Above: Sorbus arranensis.

Left: A view of Glen Diomhan reveals the precarious location of these whitebeams.

The Kelburn Weeping Larch

Location: Next to the walled garden, or 'Plaisance', of Kelburn Castle, off the A78 road about 1.6 kilometres (1 mile) south of Largs, North Ayrshire. The grounds are managed as a country park and are open to the public for most of the year.

This outlandish specimen of European larch *(Larix decidua)* in the grounds of Kelburn Castle bears no resemblance to the elegant and graceful form normally associated with the species. Said to have been planted about 1800, the 'weeping larch' occupies a prime position in the castle gardens, which overlook the Firth of Clyde south of Largs, North Ayrshire.

The tree sports a mass of twisting and contorted branches, many of considerable size, which radiate from the short, squat bole and weep to the ground. They proceed to grow haphazardly along the surface for many metres, arching and twisting and throwing up

new shoots as they go. Several branches have successfully layered to produce new trees, which in turn are starting to weep and layer, thereby perpetuating the process. Increasing in ever-expanding circles of serpentine branches, this one tree covers almost half an acre.

A fascinating old tree, the Kelburn larch is undoubtedly a mutant monster of the arboricultural world, and unique in Scotland. However, it is not without considerable character and charm, and is well worth a visit to marvel at its crazy architecture and relentless survival strategy.

The Kelburn Yews

Within the plaisance, or walled garden, of Kelburn Castle, near Largs, Ayrshire, stands a pair of yews *(Taxus baccata)* reputed to be 1000 years old. The trees, a male and a female, stand side by side 20 metres (64 feet) apart.

Location: In the walled garden of Kelburn Castle, off the A78 road about 1.2 kilometres (1 mile) south of Largs, North Ayrshire. The grounds are managed as a country park and are open to the public throughout most of the year.

They are both fine specimens with large boles measuring 5.02 metres (16 feet 6 inches) and 5.18 metres (17 feet) in girth. The branches of one of the trees extend down to ground level, creating a dark inner chamber. Despite the site having been continuously occupied by the Boyle family since 1140, the origin and history of the two yews remains a mystery.

Benmore Redwood Avenue

A most impressive example of an avenue of giant redwoods *(Sequoiadendron giganteum)* greets the visitor to the Benmore Botanic Garden. A single avenue of 48 trees is laid out in a perfectly straight line over a distance of 300 metres (984 feet) from the gatehouse almost to Benmore House itself. It was planted in 1863 by the then owner of Benmore estate, Piers Patrick.

The avenue is very formal and regular in its layout. Generous spacing between the trees has allowed the unimpeded development of deep, spire-like crowns typical of the species. The largest trees are now more than 50 metres (165 feet) tall and have girths of 6.40 metres (21 feet).

Location: At the entrance to Benmore Botanic Garden, off the A815 road about 11.3 kilometres (7 miles) north of Dunoon, Argyll. The garden is one of the regional gardens of the National Botanical Gardens of Scotland. Public access is available March to October.

The Strathleven House Oak

Location: Hidden from view in a small copse, about 100 metres (90 yards) south east of Strathleven House. The grounds are now part of the Vale of Leven Industrial Estate, off the A813 road between Dumbarton and Alexandria. Public access is available.

A veteran of great character, this tree boasts the largest trunk recorded for pedunculate or English oak *(Quercus robur)* in Scotland, with a girth of 8.89 metres (29 feet). Several centuries old, it is probably also one of the oldest oaks in Scotland. The huge trunk is very decayed and hollow, and the crown has been crudely topped about 3 metres (10 feet) from ground level. However, this old hulk still survives, producing healthy new growth from the cut stumps.

The tree stands close to Strathleven House, which was built in 1700 for William Cochrane, Commissioner to Parliament for Renfrew. The oak predates the house and was incorporated into its grounds.

The Balmaha Oak

This well known veteran oak *(Quercus robur)* stands in Balmaha Boatyard, on the eastern shores of Loch Lomond. It is a remarkable survivor from a by-gone age when the oak coppice industry was an important form of land management in the area. The tree clearly displays the legacy of coppicing, with three huge trunks arising at ground level. These in turn form a single, spreading canopy. The large trunks are heavily burred and gnarled and present an intriguing sight. Their collective volume is impressive, and the girth measured at ground level is an amazing 9.73 metres (31 feet 8 inches).

Location: Balmaha Boatyard, on the eastern shore of Loch Lomond, Stirlingshire. Public access is available.

The Duelling Trees

An unusual pair of old sweet chestnuts *(Castanea sativa)*, known as the 'Duelling Trees', remain at Ballencleroch Castle, nestling at the foot of Campsie Glen in East Dunbartonshire. Their name derives from their use as markers in duels. One tree collapsed many years ago and its fallen hulk lies on the ground, but its partner still enjoys good health.

Built about 1423, Ballencleroch Castle, came into the hands of James and Mary McFarlan in 1664, and it was about this time that tragedy befell the family. Their son, Hugh, was involved in a duel with a member of the Stirling family at the pair of old chestnut trees. The young Stirling was killed and Hugh McFarlan had to hastily leave the country for fear of reprisals. Legend has it that the ghost of young Stirling was seen wandering around the chestnut trees for many years.

On joining the army and working abroad, Hugh McFarlan's fortune changed for the better and he eventually returned and settled at Ballencleroch. He is said to have brought back many trees from his foreign travels and planted them in the grounds of the castle. This pair of ancient sweet chestnuts which still adorns the grounds, serves as a grim reminder of tragic events.

Location: The grounds of Ballencleroch Castle, in the hamlet of Clachan of Campsie, off the A891 road about 1.6 kilometres (1 mile) west of Lennoxtown, East Dunbartonshire. The castle is now run by the Schoenstatt Sisters of Mary as a convent and religious retreat. Access is available only with permission.

The Clachan Oak

The ancient sessile oak *(Quercus petraea)* that stands in Balfron, Stirlingshire is clearly a very old tree of some significance, and forms an interesting focal point. It once occupied the central green of an ancient hamlet known as 'The Clachan', which was ultimately to grow into the village of Balfron.

The tree was recorded in 1867 as being in a 'flourishing condition', with a girth of 4.8 metres (15 feet 9 inches) at 1.8 metres (6 feet) above the ground. At that time it was thought to be 334 years old and to have been struck by lightning 40 years before.[1] The short trunk, which is completely hollow, now measures 4.88 metres (16 feet) in girth.

An Edwardian postcard of the tree.

The most notable features of the tree are the two iron hoops that encircle its trunk. Nowadays they play a useful role in holding the hollow shell together, but originally they had a darker function. Until the end of the eighteenth century it was common practice to chain petty criminals to the oak tree, where they were subjected to merciless public ridicule. An iron collar was attached around the neck of the unfortunate victims and connected by a length of chain to the iron hoop encircling the trunk of the oak. This form of ritual humiliation was known as 'the jougs', and must have been a most unpleasant form of punishment.

Location: A small area of public open space next to the Church of Scotland and the A875 road in Balfron, Stirlingshire. Free public access is available throughout the year.

The Great Yew at Broich

One of Scotland's few layering yews *(Taxus baccata)* stands in the private grounds of Broich House, near Kippen, Stirlingshire. The single trunk, which measures an impressive 3.86 metres (12 feet 8 inches) in girth, supports an extensive, spreading canopy. The lower branches weep to the ground where they take root, continuing their outward progress in a maze of zig-zag growth. This single tree covers a vast area of ground as a result of this unusual growth habit, and its ever-expanding canopy has a circumference of 120 metres (394 feet). The dark and secluded inner 'chamber' formed by the surrounding skirt of layered foliage has a unique atmosphere and, at about eight metres (26 feet) in diameter, could readily accommodate between 20 and 30 people at one time. In good health and condition, the yew is thought to be between 600 and 1000 years old.

Little is known of the yew's origin. It has been suggested that it was planted by monks from the nearby island priory of Inchmahome (see page 74), on the Lake of Menteith, who were in possession of the property in the twelfth century.[1] Old buildings taken down near the site in the latter part of the nineteenth century apparently dated from the eleventh century, which adds some credence to this claim. [2]

Location: Private gardens next to Broich House (formerly known as Arngomery), off the B8037 road on the western edge of of Kippen, about 19 kilometres (12 miles) west of Stirling. Access is available only with permission.

Inchmahome Veterans

The thirteenth-century priory of Inchmahome, once home to a small community of Augustinian canons, nestles on a small, low-lying island in the middle of the Lake of Mentieth in Stirlingshire. Of the many fine trees on the island, the three veteran sweet chestnuts (*Castanea sativa*) steal the show in terms of antiquity and character. These heavily gnarled individuals are probably more than 400 years old. Although extensively decayed and hollow, they are still very much alive, and are the island's oldest living residents. The girth of their gnarled trunks ranges from 4.36 metres (14 feet 4 inches) to 6 metres (19 feet 8 inches). The largest of the three is known as the 'Antlered Chestnut' because the stag-headed branches resemble the antlers of a deer. [1]

The trees might well have been around when Mary, Queen of Scots paid a visit to the island in 1547. Accompanied by her mother, Mary of Guise, the four-year-old infant queen sought refuge at the priory for three weeks following the English victory at the Battle of Pinkie. A poem penned by the Reverend W M Stirling in 1815 recalls the royal visit:

'Those giant boughs that wave around
My aged hoary head,
Were then the tenants of the ground
Where walked the royal maid.'

Location: Alongside one of the walks radiating from Inchmahome Priory on an island in the Lake of Mentieth, Stirlingshire. The Priory is in the care of Historic Scotland and public access is available via a small passenger ferry most of the year, except the winter months.

The Poker Tree

An Edwardian postcard shows the poker hanging from a different part of the tree.

Location: Enclosed by low, white railings on the north side of the B829 road, at its junction with Manse Road, Aberfoyle, Stirlingshire. The tree can be readily viewed from the road.

The 'Poker Tree' is the unusual name given to a gnarled old oak in Aberfoyle, Stirlingshire. An unexceptional specimen, it is the amusing tale associated with it that marks it out as a tree of significance.

Bailie Nicol Jarvie, a colourful Glasgow magistrate and cousin of the infamous outlaw, Rob Roy MacGregor (1671 – 1734), was travelling on business in the wild Highlands. He stopped at an inn in the Clachan of Aberfoyle where, unfortunately, a truculent Highlander took exception to his presence and, drawing his sword, challenged him to a fight. The Bailie, unused to such violent encounters, tried to draw his sword but found it rusted to his scabbard through lack of use. As the fierce Highlander advanced upon him, the desperate Bailie grabbed a poker from the fire and brandished its red hot tip at his assailant. The poker set fire to the Highlander's plaid and sent him fleeing. The browbeaten Highlander later returned to concede defeat and congratulate Bailie on his guile and mettle in battle.

In memory of the Bailie's exploits, the iron poker was later hung from the branches of the old oak tree that stood outside the inn, and became a tourist attraction. Some years ago the poker was removed for safe-keeping. It was then thought to have been lost, but subsequently reappeared.

Robert The Bruce's Yew

A 1920s postcard shows the tree with Loch Lomond in the background.

Perched on a rocky outcrop on the western shore of Loch Lomond is an ancient yew *(Taxus baccata)* associated with King Robert the Bruce. Legend has it that The Bruce took shelter from pursuing enemies under the evergreen canopy, entertaining his troops with tales of valour. Bruce and 200 of his followers welcomed the rest, having spent a whole night and day ferrying themselves across the loch in a single leaky rowing boat which could only hold three men at a time. [1]

J C Loudon (1783 – 1843), the influential Scottish writer who chronicled changes in garden design in the early part of the nineteenth century, paid a visit to The Bruce's yew on his travels. In 1837 he recorded the girth of the trunk at ground level to be 3.96 metres (13 feet) and the height at 12.0 metres (39 feet). By 1998 the girth had increased to 6.09 metres (20 feet) and the height reduced to 5.5 metres (18 feet) as a result of heavy pruning in the interim. This suggests an annual ring width of two millimetres, a reasonable rate of increment for a slow-growing species in such a harsh environment. Now past its prime, this old campaigner must be a mere shadow of its former self, yet new sprouts of fresh growth bode well for its future.

Location: On private land near Tarbet, Argyll.

The Mightiest Conifer in Europe

The silver fir *(Abies alba)* is a native of central Europe, the Alps and the Pyrenees. The species was introduced into the United Kingdom about the beginning of the seventeenth century and the earliest trees recorded are two mentioned by Evelyn as "being planted by Serjeant Newdigate in Harefield Park in 1603".[1] Although mountains are its natural environment, the species thrives throughout the UK.

This specimen is thought to be more than 250 years old, and even in 1881 it was recorded as a huge tree. Mr Wilkie, the estate forester, calculated that it contained 56 tonnes (57 tons) of timber and said that "no true conception of this noble tree can be formed from reading a description of it".[2]

About 1910, after a visit by Charles Sargent, once dubbed "the greatest living authority on trees", Niall Diarmid Campbell (10th Duke of Argyll) wrote to the daughter of the owner of Ardkinglas saying: "It is undeniably the mightiest conifer, if not the biggest bole, of any kind in Europe." Indeed, with a girth of 9.4 metres (31 feet), this colossal silver fir tends to stop people in their tracks.

In 1906 the eminent botanist H J Elwes said that he had "never seen anything surpassing it in bulk, even in the virgin forests of Bosnia".[3] This magnificent silver fir is still thriving and will probably continue growing for many years to come.

Location: Ardkinglas Woodland Garden at Cairndow, Argyll, off the A83 Loch Lomond to Inveraray road on the eastern shores of Loch Fyne. The garden is open all year during daylight hours. Admission charges apply.

The Ardkinglas Grand Fir

Location: Ardkinglas Woodland Garden at Cairndow, Argyll, off the A83 Loch Lomond to Inveraray road on the eastern shores of Loch Fyne. The garden is open all year during daylight hours. Admission charges apply.

This majestic grand fir *(Abies grandis)* dominates Ardkinglas Woodland Garden, overlooking the shores of Loch Fyne. A native of the Pacific slopes of western North America, the species was discovered in 1825 by the Scots explorer and botanist David Douglas, who introduced it to the United Kingdom in 1831. This Ardkinglas specimen was planted in 1875, when this outstanding collection of conifers was established by the Callander family, then owners of the Argyllshire estate.

Until 1990 the tree enjoyed the distinction of being the tallest in the United Kingdom. However, at a height of 61.0 metres (200 feet), it now lies third, behind Douglas firs at Reelig Glen and Dunans in Argyll, both 62 metres (203 feet) tall. [1]

It did not take long for the Ardkinglas tree to establish its credentials as a record breaker. By 1931, at a mere 56 years old, it was already 30.48 metres (100 feet) tall and had a girth of 3.36 metres (11 feet). With no let-up in its growth rate, it took only another 53 years to surpass the 60-metre (200 feet) mark, the first tree known to have done so in the UK. The tree's perfectly clean, 'gun barrel' trunk now measures 6.22 metres (20 feet 5 inches) in girth.

Inveraray Castle Lime Avenue

Perhaps the oldest lime *(Tilia x europaea)* avenue in Scotland, according to estate records, is that at Inveraray Castle, ancestral home of the Dukes of Argyll. Thought to have been planted about 1650, several of the original trees survive to this day. The avenue has become rather fragmented over the years as trees have been lost and the resulting gaps filled by various phases of replanting. However, the overall impact of this formal style of planting still survives forming an impressive feature within the extensive policies of the castle. The original trees have huge girths and are densely shrouded in a forest of basal suckers, which make accurate measurement impossible. They are in remarkably good health, despite the length of time they have had to withstand the harsh Argyll climate.

Lime became widely planted in Scotland from the early eighteenth century, its reliability of establishment and regularity of growth making it particularly suitable for avenue planting. Avenues of lime quickly became de rigueur for the discerning landowner, especially during the Victorian era, and most country houses boast such a feature today. It is in this formal layout that most limes are encountered, where they form some of the most striking features in designed landscapes.

Location: Along an avenue running north west of Inveraray Castle, off the A83 road on the north western shore of Loch Fyne, at Inveraray, Argyll. Public access is available.

The Wishing Tree

This lone, wind-blasted hawthorn *(Crataegus monogyna)* growing in the wilds of Argyll is one of the few known 'wishing trees' in Scotland. It is encrusted with coins that have been pressed into the thin bark by generations of superstitious travellers over the centuries, each coin representing a wish. Every available space on the main trunk bristles with money, even the smaller branches and exposed roots. This magical tree provides a living connection with the ancient folklore and customs of Scotland.

Hawthorn as a species is deeply enshrined in the tradition and mythology of the British Isles. In pagan times it was regarded as the prime symbol of fertility and was celebrated as a powerful harbinger of spring. It was also strongly bound with the ancient rites of Mayday, the blossoms of 'the May' symbolising love and betrothal. Not surprisingly, hawthorn was the traditional tree used in marriages (see the Polwarth Thorn, page 30), and was also thought to possess strong healing and magical qualities.

Why a nondescript hawthorn in the Argyll wilderness has assumed such superstitious significance is lost in the mists of time. It has undoubtedly been revered as a special tree for many years, as its substantial hoard of cash will testify. Unfortunately the tree has succumbed to its harsh environment and is now lying in its enclosure.

Location: By a rough moorland track about 3.2 kilometres (2 miles) south of Ardmaddy House, near the bridge over the Atlantic to the Isle of Seil, Argyll.

Lady Miller's Beech

The fine, open-grown beech *(Fagus sylvatica)* that stands next to the old coach road between Auchtermuchty and Perth is known as 'Lady Miller's Beech'. 'Lady Miller' ran a tavern at Broomhall and was renowned for the illicit still she operated from a nearby cave, using the pure water of a natural well. Her hospitality was acclaimed by drovers and travellers, and her illegal spirits were smuggled into Perth on a regular basis. Nothing now survives of the inn, but the solitary beech tree stands as a living memorial to this colourful character. [1] The trunk measures 3.39 metres (11 feet 2 inches) in girth and the windswept crown is 19.3 metres (63 feet 4 inches) tall.

Location: Alongside a minor road midway between Auchtermuchty and Perth, close to Broomhall. The tree is on land owned by the Forestry Commission Scotland and there is public access at all times

St Andrews Holm Oak

The holm oak *(Quercus ilex)* was first introduced to the United Kingdom about 1500, but there are few good examples in Scotland. One that does continue to thrive is the fine, open-grown specimen that graces the

Location: The quadrangle of St Mary's College, St Andrews University, St Andrews, Fife. Public access is available off the main street.

quadrangle at St Mary's College, St Andrews. Thought to have been planted about 1740, its short trunk has attained a girth of 3.67 metres (12 feet), the largest recorded for this species in Scotland. The shapely crown has been heavily pruned following recent storm damage, but it is recovering well and putting on vigorous new growth. This stately tree forms a striking central feature within this ancient seat of learning.

Queen Mary's Thorn

The ancient hawthorn *(Crataegus monogyna)* that graces the Quadrangle of St Mary's College at St Andrews University is reputed to have been planted in 1563 by Mary, Queen of Scots during one of her many visits to the town. This small tree certainly possesses character and an air of importance, sitting as it does at the heart of a famous seat of learning and having a Royal provenance.

All that remains of the original tree is a decayed stump that is disintegrating badly. Judging by the size of this remnant, the tree must have had a considerable girth for its species. However, this veteran is still very much alive, three relatively young stems arising, phoenix style, from the base of the old stump to form a full and healthy crown. This living link with one of Scotland's most famous historical figures thus continues to survive, producing new and vigorous growth from the shattered hulk of the original tree.

Location: The quadrangle of St Mary's College, St Andrews University, St Andrews, Fife. Public access is available off the main street.

The Balmerino Sweet Chestnut

The peaceful ruins of Balmerino Abbey lie on the rural coast of north Fife. In the grounds of the Abbey grows an ancient sweet chestnut *(Castanea sativa)*, remarkable for its size and form. The massive trunk, with characteristically twisted grain, displays huge, bulbous swellings, and the two main limbs almost appear to wrap around each other. Although it is certainly of great age, the tree is in remarkably good condition and continues to thrive.

This sweet chestnut also has an intriguing royal provenance, because it has been closely linked to two Scottish queens. One tradition claims that the sweet chestnut was planted by Queen Ermengarde at the foundation of the Abbey in 1229, but a more plausible explanation is that it was planted by Mary, Queen of Scots in 1565 during a two-day visit to the Abbey. Tests carried out by the National Trust for Scotland in 1979 confirmed the tree to be between 390 and 425 years old, adding credence to this claim.

If it was indeed planted by Mary in 1565, it is the second oldest sweet chestnut in the United Kingdom with a known planting date, the oldest being at Castle Leod (see 1550 Chestnut, page 152).

An Edwardian postcard of the tree.

Location: The grounds of Balmerino Abbey, Balmerino, about 4.8 kilometres (3 miles) west of Newport-on-Tay, Fife, on the southern shore of the Firth of Tay. The abbey is owned by the National Trust for Scotland and access is available throughout the year. There is an honesty box for donations.

King James VI Sycamore

A wood engraving of Scone Palace in 1823 by J P Neale. One of the trees to the right of the building may well be the King James VI Sycamore.

The strong connections between Scone Palace and royalty are reflected in the many commemorative trees that grace the well kept gardens and grounds, a tradition continued to this day. One of the finest is the huge old sycamore *(Acer pseudoplatanus)* reputed to have been planted by King James VI of Scotland and I of England in 1617, during his long-awaited 'hamecoming'. This was his only visit to his homeland following the Union of the Scottish and English Crowns in 1603. James also planted an oak, which still survives.

The sycamore is a majestic specimen. Four huge limbs emerge from the short, squat trunk at between 2 metres and 3 metres (6 feet 6 inches and 10 feet) from ground level to form a vast, spreading canopy of good shape. Its trunk measures 5.50 metres (18 feet) in girth, taken at 0.3 metres (1 foot) below large swellings where the main limbs arise, and it is 21.3 metres (70 feet) tall. In 1883 its girth was recorded at 3.64 metres (12 feet) at 1.2 metres (4 feet) above the ground, and its height at 24.4 metres (80 feet).[1] The loss of one of the main limbs in a storm in 2002 has left the tree somewhat unbalanced.

Location: On the terrace close to the south east corner of Scone Palace, a short distance north of Perth on the A93 road to Braemar. The house and grounds are normally open from Good Friday to mid-October and admission charges apply. Tours are available in winter by prior appointment with the estate office.

This magnificent tree was grown from seed brought back from the Pacific north west of North America by celebrated Scottish botanist and explorer David Douglas – hence its name. Most likely the seed was collected in 1825 from the lower reaches of the Columbia River, near Fort Vancouver, arriving in Britain in 1827. The seeds were sown, the seedlings raised in a nursery and then planted out at Scone in 1834, the year that Douglas was killed on the slopes of Mauna Kea, Hawaii, when he fell into a wild cattle trap. He is buried at Kawaiahoa Church, Honolulu. Elwes [1] said that, "the tree was transplanted to its current position in 1850."

Douglas was born within the grounds of Scone Palace and worked there as a gardener. In 1820 he was accepted for a post at the Botanic Gardens, Glasgow, under Dr William Hooker, and he began his plant-hunting expeditions in 1823. Among his other discoveries are the noble and grand firs and the Sitka spruce, now widely recognised as one of the United Kingdom's most important timber trees.

Grown from the first seed to arrive in Britain and planted close to his birthplace, this Douglas fir *(Pseudotsuga menziesii)* is a living memorial to a great plant hunter whose discoveries shaped much of the commercial forest landscape of Britain.

Location: Next to the ruins of the old village of Scone, in the grounds of Scone Palace, a short distance north of Perth on the A93 road to Braemar. The house and grounds are normally open from Good Friday to mid-October and admission charges apply. Tours are available in winter by prior appointment with the estate office.

The Scone Douglas Fir

The King of the Forest

Standing majestically on the northern edge of Muirward Wood near New Scone, Perthshire, the monolithic Scots pine *(Pinus sylvestris)* known as the 'King of the Forest' lives up to its regal title.

With a girth of 6.09 metres (20 feet), this pine boasts the largest trunk recorded for this species in the United Kingdom. Its vertical growth is equally impressive at 31 metres (102 feet). Towering above the surrounding plantation, this mighty 'named' tree is an outstanding example of Scotland's native pine.

The tree forks into three trunks of roughly equal size at two metres (6 feet 6 inches) from ground level. These rise skywards almost parallel with each other to form a single canopy of good shape. The lower branches have been suppressed and must have died off early in the life of the tree, the pinkish hue of the deeply fissured bark being clearly visible around these scars.

The tree was already regarded as a novelty in the late nineteenth century. In 1883 it was recorded as being about 300 years old, 24.4 metres (80 feet) tall and 4.88 metres (16 feet) in girth.[1] At that time its triumvirate of huge trunks were calculated to contain 11.3 cubic metres (400 cubic feet) of timber.

Location: Muirward Wood, about 3.2 kilometres (2 miles) north of New Scone, Perthshire. The tree is very difficult to find amidst a maze of forest tracks. Public access is available via footpaths from New Scone.

The Pepperwell Oak

Location: The private grounds of Methven Castle, off the A85 road about 1.6 kilometres (1 mile) east of Methven, Perthshire. Access is available only with permission.

This celebrated English or pedunculate oak tree *(Quercus robur)* stands in the private grounds of Methven Castle, Perthshire. Taking its unusual name from a nearby spring, it is an imposing specimen with a girth of 7.16 metres (23 feet 6 inches) and a height of 23.8 metres (78 feet). Several centuries old, this tree has been well known in the area since the eighteenth century. In 1722 the princely sum of 100 Scottish 'merks' was offered for the tree. The oak was also described as being of "great picturesque beauty" in 1837, and "...in every respect a noble specimen of the brave old oak" in 1883.[1] Tradition also reports that a stone lies at the centre of the trunk.

Location: Private woodland close to Lynedoch Cottage in the Almond Valley, part of Scone estate, about 3.2 kilometres (2 miles) north of Methven, Perthshire. The trees are difficult to locate, and access is available only with permission.

The Mother & Father Trees

David Douglas introduced the fir that bears his name to these shores in 1827 (see page 96). Only a handful of these first trees survive, including the 'Mother and Father Trees', at Lynedoch, Scone. Until about 1861 this pair of Douglas firs *(Pseudotsuga menziesii)* supplied much of the early seed for plantings that ultimately changed the face of Scottish forestry. Such was the demand for their seed that between 1845 and 1853 the Lynedoch trees realised £500.[1] One tree measures 6.03 metres (19 feet 10 inches) in girth by 40.0 metres (131 feet) in height, and the other 6.15 metres (20 feet 3 inches) in girth and 48.5 metres (159 feet) in height.

Eppie Callum's Oak

The handsome oak in the Perthshire town of Crieff is known affectionately as 'Eppie Callum's Oak'. Several centuries old, it is said to have played a role in Scotland's turbulent history, sheltering both Rob Roy Macgregor (1671 – 1734) and Bonnie Prince Charlie (1720 – 1788) from their enemies.

The tree takes its name from a local worthy who ran the Oakbank Inn, a favourite hostelry with cattle drovers from the Highlands. Records confirm that there was indeed an old crone named Eppie Callum resident in Crieff, although it would appear that she was born long after the oak is said to have taken root. Regardless of this historical discrepancy, Eppie's name remains associated with the tree to this day.

The inimitable Dundee poet, William McGonagall (1825 – 1902), mentioned the tree in his poem, 'Beautiful Crieff':

> 'Then there's Lady Mary's Walk near the Bridge of Turret,
> Which I hope visitors will go and see and not forget,
> Because nearby grows a magnificent oak most lovely to see,
> Which is known by the name of Eppie Callum's Tree.'

Measuring 24 metres (79 feet) tall and with an impressive girth of 5.65 metres (18 feet 7 inches), this well known 'named' tree is a prominent sight in the local street scene.

An Edwardian postcard showing the tree from behind with an adjacent building (no longer standing).

Location: A private garden at the junction of Laggan Road and Turretbank Road, Crieff, Perthshire. It can readily be viewed from the public road.

LAGGAN RD

The Monzie Larch

Location: By the lake in the private garden of Monzie Castle, about 3.2 kilometres (2 miles) north of Crieff, Perthshire. Monzie Castle is open to the public on a limited number of days each year.

This 'champion' European larch *(Larix decidua)* has the largest girth so far recorded for its species in the United Kingdom. Situated at Monzie Castle, near Crieff, Perthshire it boasts an impressive girth of 6.03 metres (19 feet 10 inches) and a height of 35 metres (115 feet). It might even be the biggest of its type in the world, because only one other, in the Italian Tyrol, is reputed to be as big.[1]

The tree is one of six seedlings brought from the Tyrol in 1737 by Colonel John Menzies of Glen Lyon, Perthshire. On his way to deliver the new species to the Duke of Atholl at Dunkeld, he broke his journey at Monzie Castle. Tradition says the larches were either stolen from his hamper, or were given to the Laird of Monzie in return for his hospitality.[2]

The Hermitage Douglas

Location: On the banks of the River Braan at the Hermitage, near Dunkeld, Perthshire. The Hermitage is sign-posted off the A9, and the tree is sign-posted and readily viewed from the National Trust For Scotland property on the north side of the river. The tree is on land owned by the Forestry Commission Scotland and free public access is available throughout the year.

At a towering 59 metres (194 feet) tall, the graceful Douglas fir *(Pseudotsuga menziesii)* at the Hermitage, near Dunkeld, Perthshire, is one of the tallest trees in the United Kingdom. It nestles at the bottom of a steep gorge, with its roots in the turbulent River Braan. It is an elegant specimen, with a single, slender trunk and spire-shaped crown in perfect form to the tip of its leading shoot.

It is thought that the tree began life about 1875 as a self-sown seedling from the grove of older specimens on the opposite bank of the river. Its relatively young age makes its impressive vertical growth all the more remarkable.

Location: Alongside the footpath that runs west of the main (north) car park in Dunkeld and skirts the edge of Dunkeld Cathedral, where the path meets the woodland on the edge of the grounds of the Hilton Dunkeld House Hotel, 24 kilometres (15 miles) north of Perth. Free public access is available.

The Parent Larch

The Dunkeld Larches
by G W Wilson,
from The Larch
by C Y Michie, 1882.

With a girth of 5.6 metres (18 feet 6 inches), this is one of the largest European larches *(Larix decidua)* in the United Kingdom. It was planted after a visit to Dunkeld by a "Mr Menzies of Megeny in Glenlyon, who in 1738 brought a few small larch plants in his portmanteau, five of which he left for Duke James of Atholl."[1] Of those five, one was cut by the gardener about 1790 "by mistake",[1] and two were felled in 1809. The present tree is the last of the original five planted by Duke James. His successors, notably the 4th Duke (John, 1755 - 1830), known as the Planting Duke, were increasingly absorbed with planting European larch on the hills of Atholl. By 1830 the total planted by all the Dukes just exceeded 14 million larch trees covering nearly 4,250 hectares (10,500 acres).[1]

This tree (and its now dead companions) had already been dubbed the "Parent Larches" by 1812 [2] because they provided some of the seed for the early plantings. It now stands as a monument to the tree-planting feats achieved by the Dukes and, although an old tree, it is still a magnificent specimen.

Location: On the hillside behind Dunkeld House Hotel, Dunkeld, Perthshire. Access is available with permission of the hotel.

The Dunkeld Pedestal Larch

Only two examples of so-called 'pedestal larch' *(Larix decidua)* are known to exist in Scotland. The prefix 'pedestal' refers to the tree's shape when a perfectly normal-looking tree grows up from a vastly swollen and contorted base. The distinction between the normal tree and the base tends to be very obvious, giving the impression that the trunk is growing out of a raised pedestal. The 'pedestal' consists of a twisted mass of roots that almost appears to be 'corkscrewing' the tree out of the ground.

One theory as to how such trees arise is that they were propagated in a container and retained within a restricted environment for many years, thus becoming 'pot-bound', with distorted roots. Once planted out, the pressures exerted by the downward spiral of the deformed root system gradually forced the root ball out of the ground.

The best example of this eccentric growth habit stands on a wooded hillside behind Dunkeld House Hotel. Its pedestal stands at a height of 1.2 metres (4 feet) and has a girth of 7.88 metres (25 feet 10 inches). This narrows abruptly and the normal trunk that emerges from it has the much reduced girth of 5.02 metres (16 feet 6 inches). The tree is thought to be of considerable age, dating from between 1720 and 1740.

The Original Japanese Larches

The Japanese larch *(Larix kaempferi)* was first introduced to British shores in 1861 by the eminent Victorian plant collector and botanist, Henry Veitch. However, it was not until 26 years later that the 7th Duke of Atholl expressed an interest in what was a new and untried species. On returning from a visit to Japan in 1885, he brought seed with him from the country's indigenous larch and planted 14 trees in 1887, near Dunkeld House. These trees survive to this day, 11 of them forming a shallow crescent lining the driveway.

The success of the early plantings at Dunkeld was largely responsible for the Japanese larch's meteoric rise to prominence as one of Scotland's principal forest species. It is now widely planted as a timber tree and has become one of the mainstays of the country's commercial forestry industry, having an ability to grow rapidly over a wider range of site conditions than its European cousin *(Larix decidua)*. It is also resistant to larch canker, a serious and damaging disease of the European species.

As well as representing the early pioneers of the species in Scotland, the Dunkeld trees are notable as the parents of the first hybrid larch *(Larix x eurolepis)*, first recognised in 1904.

Location: The trees form a shallow crescent on the north side of the private driveway serving Dunkeld House Hotel, Dunkeld, Perthshire. Public access and an interpretation panel are available.

The Dunkeld Douglas

The Douglas fir *(Pseudotsuga menziesii)* with the largest girth recorded in the United Kingdom stands close to Dunkeld Cathedral. Despite an impressive girth of 7.0 metres (23 feet), it is easily overlooked because it is located in a woodland containing many fine trees of great size.

Said to have been planted as a gift to the Duke of Atholl about 1846, it is coarsely branched and not particularly attractive. Its top was blown out many years ago, and it now stands at just over 30 metres (98 feet) tall. The bark on the lower trunk is exceptionally thick and deeply fissured, a characteristic that undoubtedly contributes to its vast bulk.

Location: A small woodland immediately west of Dunkeld Cathedral, Dunkeld, Perthshire. Public access is available throughout the year via a footpath.

Location: On the south bank of the River Tay at the Perthshire village of Birnam, reached via a sign-posted footpath from Dunkeld bridge and another from the Birnam House Hotel in the centre of the village. Free public access is available throughout the year.

The Birnam Sycamore

Almost as famous as its near neighbour, the Birnam Oak (see page 114), the mighty sycamore *(Acer pseudoplatanus)* growing on the fertile banks of the Tay is an impressive sight. Thought to be more than 300 years old, it appears to be an out-grown pollard that now supports a huge, spreading, dome-shaped crown typical of the species. Particularly remarkable are its buttress roots, which seem to mould themselves to the bank of the River Tay.

The tree's girth has been regularly measured over the years and shows steady and vigorous growth: 6.1 metres (20 feet) in 1906, 6.7 metres (22 feet) in 1956, 7.1 metres (23 feet 4 inches) in 1981 and 7.62 metres (25 feet) in 1998.

The Birnam Oak

William Shakespeare
(1564 – 1616)

An ancient sessile oak *(Quercus petraea)* standing on the banks of the River Tay near the village of Birnam is said to be the last survivor of the legendary Birnam Wood, immortalised in Shakespeare's Macbeth:

> 'Macbeth shall never vanquish'd be until
> Great Birnam Wood to high Dunsinane Hill
> Shall come against him.'

The witches' prophecy literally came true, when Malcolm's army camouflaged itself with branches from the great wood and took by surprise Macbeth's stronghold at Dunsinane, 20 kilometres (12 miles) to the south east:

> 'As I did stand my watch upon the hill,
> I looked toward Birnam and anon methought
> The wood began to move.'

The tragic Macbeth then meets his gruesome end.

Location: On the south bank of the River Tay at Birnam, Perthshire, accessible via a sign-posted footpath from Dunkeld bridge and another from the Birnam House Hotel in the centre of the village. Free public access is available throughout the year.

It is unlikely that this fine old veteran, sometimes known as 'Macbeth's Oak', was around to furnish Malcolm's soldiers with greenery when the battle was reputedly fought, in 1057. It is, however, several centuries old and represents a living relic of the great medieval oakwood that once clothed the banks of the Tay.

The trunk boasts an impressive girth of 5.5 metres (18 feet) and a widely spreading canopy composed of long, horizontal limbs. A stately survivor of a bygone age, its literary connection has resulted in its becoming one of Scotland's better-known heritage trees.

Location: Alongside the A93 trunk road about 6.4 kilometres (4 miles) south of Blairgowrie, Perthshire. Parking and an interpretation board are available.

The Meikleour Beech Hedge

Since 1966, the impressive beech *(Fagus sylvatica)* hedge that runs adjacent to the busy A93 road has been officially recognised as the tallest in the world. This over-powering 'green wall' stands 36.6 metres (120 feet) tall at its northern end and gradually diminishes to a mere 24.4 metres (80 feet) at its southern extremity, with an average height of 30 metres (100 feet). About 530 metres (1738 feet) long, it is cut and re-measured every 10 years, a complex operation that takes four men about six weeks to complete.

An Edwardian postcard of the hedge.

The hedge is believed to have been laid out and planted in the autumn of 1745, the year of the second Jacobite uprising, by Jean Mercer and her husband, Robert Murray Nairne. Following the death of her husband at the battle of Culloden a year later, Jean Mercer moved to Edinburgh to live with friends, leaving the young hedge to grow untended. A more romantic version of events has it that the gardeners who planted the hedge took up arms for Bonnie Prince Charlie and perished on the field of Culloden. Their hedge was left to grow untended towards the heavens as a living monument to their memory. Whatever the explanation for its great height, the hedge is now a world-beating wonder and a popular attraction for tourists.

The Camperdown Elm

The Camperdown elm *(Ulmus glabra* 'Camperdownii'*)* is a natural mutant of Scotland's native wych elm. It was discovered by chance about 1835 growing wild in woodland by the Earl of Camperdown's head forester, David Taylor. Intrigued by its alien appearance, Taylor carefully lifted and transplanted the tree to the landscaped grounds that surround Camperdown House, on the outskirts of Dundee. Before long, interest in this outlandish variety grew and the Camperdown elm provided the early cuttings from which it was to be widely propagated. The instantly recognisable form of the tree soon became a common sight in parks, gardens and cemeteries.

The original tree survives to this day, and has so far escaped the ravages of Dutch elm disease. Standing no more than 3 metres (10 feet) tall, the weeping branches extend to the ground. However, it is the bizarre branch architecture that is its most remarkable feature. The crown consists of a mass of heavily convoluted and twisted branches knotted together in dense clusters. These painfully and impossibly double back repeatedly on one another to create a marvellous living sculpture unrivalled by any other variety of tree.

Location: Camperdown Park, on the north western outskirts of Dundee. It is owned and managed by Dundee City Council and free public access is available at all times.

The Dibble Tree

Edwardian postcard revealing how little the tree has grown in the last century.

This quaint title belongs to a willow *(Salix alba* 'caerulea'*)* growing near the centre of Carnoustie, Angus. A tree of great local significance, it is said to have originated from a 'dibble', or planting stick, absent-mindedly left in the ground in 1797 by Tammas Lousen (Thomas Lowson), an itinerant shipwright and salmon fisher. As the tree took root and began to grow, he decided to settle down and build a house. Others came to join him, and soon the solitary willow tree became a symbol of their community. From this humble beginning as a small coastal crofting community, Carnoustie grew into the popular holiday and golfing resort it is today. The willow tree still stands, a living tribute to the town's founding father.

The tree is of no great size for its reputed age, with a girth of only 1.73 metres (5 feet 8 inches) and a height of 10.5 metres (34 feet). The elements have not been kind, and the tree was apparently split in two by a lightning strike in the mid-eighteenth century. However, regular pruning has maintained a healthy flush of foliage each year.

The tree was restored by Angus Council as part of the Burgh's bicentennial celebrations in 1997.

Location: Next to the public toilets on a small lane off Ferrier Street, 50 metres (55 yards) south of the town centre. It is well sign-posted. Free public access is available throughout the year.

Glamis Horse Chestnut

Glamis Castle, the childhood home of Queen Elizabeth the Queen Mother, has been a royal residence since 1372. In front of the castle stands a fine old horse chestnut *(Aesculus hippocastanum)*, said to have been a favourite of the Queen Mother.

Location: The lawn in front of Glamis Castle, near Forfar, Angus. The castle is open to the public from April until October. Admission charges apply.

An open-grown specimen, it is recorded as being planted in 1746. It has large, heavy limbs that radiate from the short trunk and descend to the ground. The resulting ring of greenery forms a secluded enclosure. In 1884 the tree was already large, the trunk measuring 3 metres (9 feet 10 inches) in girth and 16.8 metres (55 feet) in height. By 1999, the girth had increased to 4.17 metres (13 feet 9 inches) and the height to 20.3 metres (67 feet).

Neil Gow's Oak

Neil Gow (1727 – 1807), a famous Scottish fiddler, supposedly composed many of Scotland's best-loved strathspeys and reels in the shade of this old sessile oak *(Quercus petraea)* that grows on the banks of the River Tay, near Dunkeld. The tree that now bears his name is also known as the 'Fiddle Tree', and stands in living memory of this colourful character. The Gow family brought folk music into a new professional era in the 1770s, encouraged by the Duke of Atholl.

The gnarled old trunk of the oak measures 5.84 metres (19 feet) in girth and the crown reaches 21.8 metres (71 feet) in height. The bole is heavily decayed and the roots grip tenaciously to the steep riverbank.

Location: The southern bank of the River Tay, accessible by public footpath from the bridge at Dunkeld, Perthshire. The tree is on land owned by the Forestry Commission Scotland and public access is available at all times.

The Birks of Aberfeldy

The birches *(Betula spp.)* that clothe the deep glen formed by the Moness Burn, to the south of Aberfeldy, became nationally famous following a visit in 1787 by the nation's bard, Robert Burns. So impressed was he with the natural beauty of the area that he was inspired to write one of his well known works, "The Birks o' Aberfeldie":

> 'Now simmer blinks on flow'ry braes,
> And o'er the crystal streamlets plays,
> Come let us spend the lightsome days
> In the birks of Aberfeldie!'

As a result, the glen has been maintained as a scenic walk for more than 200 years and the birch trees have become internationally famous.

Location: Moness Glen, south of Aberfeldy, Perthshire, with access off the A826 road. The glen is owned and maintained by Perth and Kinross Council and free public access is available throughout the year.

Monster Red Cedar

A native of the north west American seaboard, western red cedar *(Thuya plicata)* was introduced to the United Kingdom in 1853 by William Lobb (1809 – 1863). A most remarkable specimen stands in a private estate near Aberfeldy, Perthshire. Many large limbs arise at ground level from the original tree and these spread out and layer to form an ever-increasing circle of new trees. This in turn has created a huge grove of twisted and bowed trunks that cover a huge area. Many of the individual trunks are very large, and the volume of timber in this one breathtaking specimen must be equivalent to the timber content of a small woodland.

Location: The private grounds of Findynate House, on the north bank of the River Tay near Aberfeldy, Perthshire. Access is available only with permission.

Diana's Grove

Diana's Grove, in the grounds of Blair Castle, is an outstanding collection of breathtaking conifers that have attained tremendous size. The grove was established between 1872 and 1880 as a tribute to the Roman goddess of hunting. Many trees exceed 45 metres (150 feet) in height, and the Grove contains several of the largest trees in the United Kingdom.

The noble fir *(Abies procera)*, which is tree number 11 in the grove, is a superb specimen with a clean, straight trunk for the first 10 metres (30 feet). Its overall height is 50 metres (165 feet) and the trunk has a girth of 3.96 metres (13 feet). This handsome species was discovered and introduced by David Douglas in 1830.

Location: The grounds of Blair Castle, off the A9 about 56 kilometres (35 miles) north of Perth. The castle and grounds are open to the public. Admission charges apply.

Location: Cluny Garden, sign-posted off an unclassified road along the north bank of the River Tay, about 4 kilometres (3.5 miles) east of Aberfeldy, Perthshire. Public access is available and admission charges apply.

The Cluny Redwood

Since its introduction to Scotland in 1853 by John Matthew of Perthshire, the giant redwood *(Sequoiadendron giganteum)* has become an instantly recognisable feature in the Scottish landscape. Its elegant spire invariably towers above surrounding trees or stands aloof in policies and parkland. The giant redwood grows extremely rapidly in the Scottish climate and relatively young trees have already reached tremendous size, none more so than the vast specimen at Cluny Garden, near Aberfeldy, Perthshire. With a girth of 11.05 metres (36 feet 3 inches), the largest recorded for any tree in Scotland, this mightily impressive 'champion' dominates all around it.

Wood engraving of the tree
from "Sylva Britannica"
by J.G. Strutt (1830).

Location: The churchyard at Fortingall, about 13 kilometres (8 miles) west of Aberfeldy, Perthshire. Free public access is available all year.

The Fortingall Yew

Estimated to be perhaps 5,000 years old, the Fortingall Yew *(Taxus baccata)* stands at the geographical heart of Scotland. It is believed to be the most ancient tree in the United Kingdom, and is probably even the oldest living thing in Europe.

The tree was first described in 1769 by the Hon. Daines Barrington [1], who measured its circumference at 16 metres (52 feet). By July 1833 [2] Dr Neil found that large amounts had been cut away "by the country people, with the view of forming quechs or drinking cups, and other relics, which visitors were in the habit of purchasing". The trunk then resembled a semicircular wall, although new spray and a few young branches were growing to a height of up to 9 metres (30 feet).

In 1854, Loudon [3] said "its age is unknown, but it has long been a mere shell, forming an arch through which funeral processions were accustomed to pass".

Today this venerable tree is still a very impressive sight and is enclosed by a wall built to create a sanctuary for its undisturbed growth. Its trunk now comprises several separate elements and without knowing the tree's long history it would be difficult to regard it as a single tree.

The Glen Lyon Ash

Location: A private field near Slatich Farm, about 16 kilometres (10 miles) along Glen Lyon from Fortingall, near Aberfeldy. It stands close to the public road, from where it can easily be viewed.

One of the oldest examples of Scotland's native ash *(Fraxinus excelsior)* lives in Perthshire's beautiful Glen Lyon. The moss-covered trunk measures an exceptional girth of 6.40 metres (21 feet), the largest recorded for this species in Scotland. Once reaching 30 metres (98 feet) in height, the crown has been heavily cut back to a stump of about 4 metres (13 feet).

This veteran might be about 300 to 400 years old, an exceptional age for ash, which is not known as a long-lived species. Under normal circumstances in Scotland ash can be expected to reach a maximum age of 200 to 250 years before decay and decline set in.

Location: Sutherland's Grove, sign-posted off the A828 about 19 kilometres (12 miles) north of Oban, Argyll. The site is owned by the Forestry Commission Scotland and parking, an interpretation panel and free public access are available all year.

Sutherland's Grove

A fine stand of about 40 Douglas fir *(Pseudotsuga menziesii)*, known as 'Sutherland's Grove', overlooks Loch Creran at Barcaldine Forest, near Oban, Argyll. Planted about 1870, the trees stand an average 46 metres (150 feet) tall, with the tallest recorded at more than 50 metres (164 feet). Their straight, clean trunks are of equally impressive size, measuring up to 4.96 metres (16 feet 3 inches) in girth.

On a granite boulder in the heart of the grove is an inscription in memory of Sir John Donald Sutherland, Forestry Commissioner for Scotland between 1934 and 1942. His ashes are scattered among the giant firs, in the grove that bears his name.

Rannoch Rowan

An expansive view across Rannoch Moor shows the true isolation of this tree.

Surely the loneliest tree in Scotland is the rowan *(Sorbus aucuparia)* that stands in splendid isolation in the desolate wilderness of Rannoch Moor. It perches on top of a giant boulder, its windswept crown bearing testament to the extreme exposure with which it has to contend. Remarkably, the tree has managed to maintain a hold in the crevices of its lichen-encrusted pedestal, its roots somehow seeking sustenance from a deep fissure in the rock. This lonely rowan is now a well known landmark on the busy A82 road.

The secret of the tree's survival is its elevated position, which keeps it out of reach of the relentless grazing by sheep and deer. Rowan, a species native to Scotland, is an opportunist of the tree world, and this particular tree has carved out its own niche in a harsh environment.

Rannoch Moor was not always so bleak and treeless. Between 5000 and 2500 years ago, Scotland's climate was drier and more continental, causing the bogs to dry out briefly. A vast forest of birch and pine colonised the moor, only to disappear as the climate gradually changed again. All that now remains are countless stumps entombed in a peaty grave, and a small remnant of native pinewood known as the Black Wood of Rannoch.

Location: Beside the A82 trunk road between Glen Coe and Bridge of Orchy. Public access is available.

The Seven Men of Moidart

The 'Seven Men of Moidart' are a line of beech trees *(Fagus sylvatica)* that commemorate the seven companions who landed with Bonnie Prince Charlie in 1745, when he raised the standard at nearby Glenfinnan. Thought to have been planted early in the nineteenth century, only five of the original seven trees remain as living monuments to those involved in this pivotal event in Scotland's past. A severe storm in 1988 caused extensive damage to the trees, which occupy a picturesque but highly exposed Highland setting on the northern shore of Loch Moidart.

The surviving 'five men' are of great size, with huge and heavily buttressed trunks ranging in girth from 4.3 metres (14 feet) to 5.18 metres (17 feet). However, they are in poor condition and the trunks are badly decayed. These fine old veterans are living on borrowed time: the next big storm that sweeps up the glen is likely to result in more casualties. Nevertheless, the surviving 'companions' are fine old trees that commemorate an important historical occasion.

Location: About 600 metres (660 yards) south of the A861 in a private field near Kinlochmoidart, Highland. Roadside parking and an interpretation cairn are available, but access to the trees is restricted.

The Drumtochty Sitka

This giant Sitka spruce *(Picea sitchensis)* grows in Drumtochty Glen, near Fettercairn, Aberdeenshire. One of the largest-girthed examples so far recorded for this species in Scotland, it measures an impressive 6.78 metres (22 feet 3 inches) in girth. Its height is equally remarkable, at 50 metres (165 feet). It has a superb shape and is a fine example of a species that has radically changed the face of Scottish forestry.

Sitka spruce, a native of the Pacific north west of America, owes its now ubiquitous presence in the United Kingdom to a pair of pioneering Scots. Discovered by Archibald Menzies in 1792, it was introduced to these shores by the prolific plant collector David Douglas in 1832. However, it was not until the formation of the Forestry Commission in 1919 that the species received any particular attention. It soon became apparent to those charged with regenerating the United Kingdom's much depleted woodland resource that Sitka was the new 'wonder tree', thriving in the mild, wet Scottish climate and with a capacity to produce high yields on poor sites. These features rapidly endeared it to a fast-developing forest industry, and today Sitka continues to play a vital role in the nation's timber supply.

Archibald Menzies
(1754 – 1842)

Location: Alongside a Forestry Commission Scotland car park on an unclassified road that runs east from the B974 road, from a junction at Clatterin' Brig, about 4.8 kilometres (3 miles) north of Fettercairn, Aberdeenshire. An interpretation board and free public access are available throughout year.

The Twin Trees of Finzean

Growing in a small stand of pine on the Finzean Estate in Aberdeenshire, these two remarkable Scots pine trees *(Pinus sylvestris)* have formed a most unusual natural arch. Many years ago, a branch from one of the trees naturally grafted itself on to its neighbour, forever joining the two together. The 'Twin Trees', as they have become known, are an arboricultural curiosity, even featuring in old postcards of the area. Now about 100 years old, the pair of pines make a distinctive local landmark.

Location: Next to the B976 road on the eastern outskirts of the hamlet of Finzean, Aberdeenshire. The trees are readily visible from the public road.

Location: On the edge of woodland lining the private drive to Ballogie House, off the B976 road about 5.6 kilometres (3.5 miles) south east of Aboyne, Aberdeenshire. Access is available only with permission.

Queen of the Firs

One of Scotland's finest and most impressive Scots pine trees *(Pinus sylvestris)* stands at Ballogie Estate, near Aboyne, Aberdeenshire. It is known affectionately as the 'Queen of the Firs', as Scots pine used to be known as Scots fir. It is easy to see why this specimen has assumed its regal title as it is of exceptionally large size for the species, with a girth of 4.71 metres (15 feet 6 inches) and a towering height of 37 metres (121 feet). The single, straight trunk is clean and branch-free for most of its length, with a beautiful tracery of bark markings. It is recorded as being planted in 1792 and has been regularly measured over the past 100 years.

Leith Hall Dule Tree

Some of Scotland's trees have a dark and grim past. One of the best known 'dule' trees, or hanging trees, stands in the grounds of Leith Hall, near Huntly, Aberdeenshire. This tree, a sycamore *(Acer pseudoplatanus)*, was used as a natural gibbet, its strong timber being ideal for the purpose.

Leith Hall dates from about 1650 and the tree might have been planted shortly after this. A rather gaunt and heavily branched specimen, the trunk measures 3.64 metres (12 feet) in girth. There are few surviving dule trees left in Scotland, so this one provides a poignant reminder of harsher times (see also Blairquhan Dool Tree, page 12).

Location: The grounds of Leith Hall, about 5.6 kilometres (3.5 miles) north east of Rhynie, Aberdeenshire, north of the B9002. Leith Hall is owned by the National Trust for Scotland and the gardens and grounds are open all year.

The Kilravock Layering Beech

Beeches *(Fagus sylvatica)* with a tendency to layer are extremely rare in Scotland. Their low branches reach to the ground and take root, throwing up a ring of young trees around the central mother stem.

Location: On a low bank alongside the driveway to Kilravock Castle, on the B9091 road between Croy and Clephanton, approximately 16 kilometres (10 miles) east of Inverness and the A9. The castle is administered by Ellel Ministries as a hotel and religious retreat. Access is available only with permission.

Of the very few specimens known to exist, the finest and largest is that which graces the grounds of Kilravock Castle, Inverness-shire. The tree is thought to be more than 300 years old, and its huge trunk measures 4.93 metres (16 feet) in girth. It is also known as the 'Kissing Beech', after a member of the owner's family and a housemaid were witnessed in an illicit embrace under its spreading limbs.

The Darnaway Oak

The largest-girthed broadleaved tree in Scotland is a sessile oak *(Quercus petraea)* that stands in a narrow strip of ancient woodland at the Meads of St John, on Morayshire's Darnaway estate. The trunk measures an incredible 9.73 metres (31 feet) in girth. The oak is also very old, recent research using trunk diameter and core samples estimating it to be about 730 years old.[1]

This mighty 'champion' is one of several ancient oaks standing on the banks of the River Findhorn. These are thought to be survivors of the vast Royal Forest of Darnaway, which once clothed the fertile lowlands of Morayshire in medieval times. Much of the forest was felled in the Middle Ages to provide timber for ships, castles and houses, although it was still renowned for its oak at the end of the nineteenth century. Proceedings of the Royal Scottish Arboricultural Society noted in 1881:

> 'The oak forest of Darnaway is acknowledged to be the finest in Scotland, and there are few which can compare with it anywhere in the British Isles. For a century the oak produce from this forest, which is over 3000 acres in extent, has attracted attention from all over the north of Scotland...'[2]

Location: In a small area of woodland fringing the west bank of the River Findhorn at the Meads of St John on the Darnaway estate, near Forres, Morayshire. Access is available only with permission.

The Great Fraser Yew

One of Scotland's most remarkable yew trees *(Taxus baccata)* grows on the Knockie estate, at Stratherrick, near Fort Augustus. Located on the wild shores of Loch Ness in a Site of Special Scientific Interest, the tree forms a grove of about 20 stems. Uniquely, for yew, these have sprung up from root suckers that have collectively created a dense, spreading grove with a circumference of 110 metres (361 feet). The central 'mother' stem measures 4.58 metres (15 feet) at ground level. This ancient yew was traditionally the gathering point for the Clan Fraser in times of trouble. Its age is unknown, although it might be as old as 700 years.

Location: The southern bank of Loch Ness on the Knockie estate, near Fort Augustus. It is reached by a strenuous 4.8 kilometre (3 mile) walk across moorland. Access is available only with permission.

The Seer's Oak

Location: Alongside a small public road between the hamlets of Achmore and Braeintra, near the village of Stromeferry, Wester Ross. Public access is available.

The Wester Ross village of Stromeferry has a very special sessile oak tree *(Quercus petraea)*. The Brahan Seer, Coinneach (Kenneth) Odhar, prophesied in the late seventeenth century that it would be a very bad day for the people of the district if any two men could link arms around the trunk of the big oak tree. Thankfully, this has never been achieved. The oak stands out as the biggest in the area by far and the trunk, measuring 4.62 metres (15 feet) in girth, is impossible for two men to encircle.

Dughall Mor

Location: Reelig Glen, south of the A862 near Beauly, about 11.3 kilometres (7 miles) west of Inverness. Turn off the A862 towards Moniack. The Glen is owned by the Forestry Commission Scotland. Public access and car parking are available, and Dughall Mor is sign-posted on the forest walk.

The tallest tree so far recorded in the United Kingdom, and indeed Europe, is a Douglas fir *(Pseudotsuga menziesii)* in Reelig Glen, near Inverness. Planted as recently as 1882, this tall and elegant specimen has reached a staggering height of 62 metres (203 feet 5 inches). The Forestry Commission Scotland ran a competition among local people to find a name for this champion of the tree world, and have christened it Dughall Mor, which in Gaelic means 'big dark stranger'.

Dughall Mor forms part of a grove of very tall Douglas firs that comprise the largest concentration of trees exceeding 55 metres (180 feet) anywhere in the British Isles. They are so straight and tall that one was felled to provide a replacement mast for the 'Discovery', the ship in which explorer Sir Robert Scott sailed to the Antarctic (the 'Discovery' is now berthed at Dundee). This fir is obviously thriving in the fertile and sheltered environment of the glen, with a ready supply of moisture from the Moniack Burn. This deceptive champion has a relatively slender trunk and its great height is difficult to appreciate, surrounded as it is by other giants.

Springtime in Reelig Glen, with a stand of massive Douglas firs visible through the beeches.

Duncan Forbes' Oak

A most unusual pot-bellied oak stands isolated in a field overlooking the Beauly Firth west of Inverness. It takes its name from Duncan Forbes of Culloden (1685 – 1747), who was Lord President of the Court of Session during the second Jacobite uprising. He is supposed to have sat under this remarkable specimen to think and plan.

Loyal to the King, Forbes was the bane of the Jacobite cause and did much to oppose the rebels. Indeed, he was instrumental in the defeat of Bonnie Prince Charlie at the battle of Culloden (1746) and was subsequently credited as saving Scotland for the House of Hanover. Such was his power and influence at the time that he was known in the Highlands as 'King Duncan'. The 'King' is dead, but the old oak tree lives on, forever associated with this historical figure.

It is notable for its grossly swollen and distended trunk, measuring 6.28 metres (20 feet 8 inches) in girth at its widest point. The reason for the swelling is a huge burr which exaggerates its girth. Repeated browsing by the resident flock of sheep may have stimulated this unusual form of growth. At only 5 metres (16 feet) in height, this living barrel of a tree has a healthy, flat-topped crown.

Location: On private agricultural land west of Inverness.

The Fairburn Sitka

The grounds of Fairburn House, near Contin, Highland, are home to many fine trees. The most impressive is the massive Sitka spruce *(Picea sitchensis)* that dominates the lawn. The heavily branched trunk measures 7.83 metres (25 feet 8 inches) in girth and is one of the largest recorded for this species in the United Kingdom. Its height is equally impressive at 44.8 metres (147 feet).

Location: The grounds of Fairburn House, 3.2 kilometres (2 miles) south of Contin, Easter Ross. Access is gained via the A832 road. The grounds are open to the public on a limited number of days each year. At other times access is available only with permission.

The healthy foliage extends down to ground level, an unusual feature on a species normally grown in dense plantations. The Fairburn tree was probably planted shortly after the introduction of Sitka spruce by David Douglas in 1832, and is now a superb specimen of great size and character.

The Brahan Elm

The largest-girthed wych elm *(Ulmus glabra)* in the United Kingdom resides at Brahan Estate, Easter Ross. Planted in 1735, this 'champion' measured 7.03 metres (23 feet) in girth reaching a height of 25.6 metres (84 feet) in 2002. It is a fine, open-grown specimen in an area of historic parkland, and still enjoys good health, despite its exposed location. Wych elm is native to the United Kingdom and is the species of elm most commonly found in Scotland. The Brahan tree has so far escaped the ravages of Dutch elm disease, a fungus spread from tree to tree by a bark beetle.

Location: Private parkland south of Brahan House, on Brahan estate, on the south side of the A835 road about 4.8 kilometres (3 miles) west of Maryburgh, Easter Ross, Highland. Access is available only with permission.

1550 Sweet Chestnut

The tree with the oldest recorded planting date in the United Kingdom is the superb sweet chestnut *(Castanea sativa)* at Castle Leod, Strathpeffer. Estate records show the tree was planted in 1550 by John Mackenzie (1480 – 1556), 9th Chief of Kintail and a Privy Councillor to King James V and Mary, Queen of Scots.

The tree is an outstanding specimen of very large size. The long, clean trunk measures 8.10 metres (26 feet 7 inches) in girth and the lofty canopy has attained a height of 28 metres (92 feet). Historical measurements of the trunk's girth suggest a relatively slow rate of growth. In 1867 the girth was 5.53 metres (18 feet 2 inches), in 1908 6.40 metres (21 feet 6 inches), and in 1938 7.06 metres (23 feet 3 inches). The thick, fissured bark on the bole displays a strong spiral twist that is very characteristic of old sweet chestnuts. The angle of the spiral tends to increase as trees age, although the grain of the underlying timber normally remains vertical. Despite its very great age, the Castle Leod tree is in remarkably good health. Unfortunately, a second, smaller sweet chestnut also dating from 1550 was lost in a gale in 1979.

Location: The grounds of Castle Leod, off the A834 road about 0.8 kilometres (half a mile) east of Strathpeffer, Easter Ross, Highland. The grounds are open to the public at certain times throughout the year.

The Castle Leod Redwood

Location: The grounds of Castle Leod, off the A834 0.8 kilometres (half a mile) east of Strathpeffer, Easter Ross, Highland The grounds are open to the public at certain times throughout the year.

The tallest giant redwood *(Sequoiadendron giganteum)* so far recorded in the United Kingdom stands in the grounds of Castle Leod, Strathpeffer. It measures a staggering 52 metres (170 feet) tall and its equally impressive trunk has a girth of 8.92 metres (29 feet 3 inches). The tree is also notable as one of the few surviving original introductions of this species, brought to these shores by the Scottish botanist and plant collector John Matthew in 1853.

The estate records it as being planted in 1853 to commemorate the first birthday of Francis Mackenzie, Viscount Tarbat and later Earl of Cromartie. Regular measurements taken since 1891 show rapid growth. By 1954, only 100 years after planting, the tree had already topped 30 metres (98 feet) and the beautifully flared trunk had attained a girth of 6.94 metres (22 feet 9 inches). The tree is a handsome and stately specimen, with a shapely, spire-like crown so typical of the species.

The giant redwood is often referred to as 'Wellingtonia', a name given to it by John Lindley of the Horticultural Society. He thought it appropriate that the world's most impressive tree should commemorate the Duke of Wellington, who had died the year before.

The champion giant redwood may be seen to the immediate right of the castle.

The Dundonnell Yew

Location: The private garden of Dundonnell House, near Dundonnell, Wester Ross, Highland. Access is available only by permission and the garden is also open on selected days through Scotland's Garden Scheme.

This ancient and beautiful yew *(Taxus baccata)* forms the centrepiece of a private garden in Dundonnell, near Ullapool, Highland. It appears to have been coppiced many years ago and the resulting re-growth has formed a ring of interlaced stems. The huge trunk, one of the largest recorded for yew in Scotland, measures 7.0 metres (23 feet) in girth at ground level. Although there are no records of its age, the tree is certainly very old; estimates vary widely, between 600 and 2000 years. This tree is notable for another reason: it has achieved its great size despite growing at the unusually high latitude for yews of 57 degrees north.

Location: Main Street, Kirkwall, Orkney Islands. Public access is available.

The Big Tree of Orkney

Orkney's biggest and oldest tree stands in Kirkwall's Main Street. A well known local landmark, the solitary sycamore *(Acer pseudoplatanus)* is known as 'The Big Tree', because Orkney's windswept environment means that few trees can survive or grow to any appreciable size. It appears to have arisen as a windblown seedling, and is now several centuries old. Urban development has encroached heavily on the tree which is displaying symptoms of decline. The hollow trunk has been heavily cut back to a stump of about 3 metres (10 feet). However, the tree is clearly a great survivor, and has sprouted new, healthy growth from the cut stump.

The Tree Council – working together for trees

The Tree Council is a conservation charity and the UK's lead tree campaigning partnership, dedicated to inspiring, initiating and enabling effective action for trees in town and countryside. It campaigns to make more people aware that trees matter – and that effective action for trees and woods means a great deal more than just planting new ones. It also works towards more trees, of the right kind and in the right place, and better care for all trees, of all ages.

The Tree Council grew out of 1973's National Tree Year, with its slogan of "Plant a Tree in '73". It was founded the following year as an umbrella body for organisations working together for trees – planting, caring for and enjoying them – and as a forum for tackling issues relating to trees and woods. Members range from professional, non-governmental, specialist and trade organisations, including other conservation charities, to local authorities and government agencies.

Every year the Tree Council organises a series of UK-wide festivals to celebrate trees, with events planned by its members, its 7,500 volunteer Tree Wardens, and other supporters. The calendar begins with Seed Gathering Sunday on the second Sunday in October, followed by National Tree Week at the end of November to launch the planting season, Trees Love Care Days in March, and Walk in the Woods in May.

For further information visit: www.treecouncil.org.uk

Scottish Natural Heritage (SNH)

SNH is a government body, responsible to Scottish Executive Ministers, and through them to the Scottish Parliament. It works with the people to care for the natural heritage. This includes designating rare, endangered or vulnerable trees and woodland as Sites of Special Scientific Interest or Special Areas of Conservation, and providing advice on any activity that might affect the conservation of these areas.

Scotland's natural heritage is a local, national and global asset. SNH promotes its care and improvement, its responsible enjoyment, its greater understanding and appreciation, and its sustainable use now and for future generations.

SNH works in partnership, by co-operation, negotiation and consensus. Where possible, it does this with all relevant interests in Scotland: public, private and voluntary organisations, and individuals. It operates in a devolved manner, delegating decision-making to the local level within the organisation to encourage and assist SNH to be accessible, sensitive and responsive to local needs and circumstances. It operates in an open and accountable manner in all its activities.

For further information visit: www.snh.org.uk

Forestry Commission Scotland

Forestry Commission Scotland is part of the Forestry Commission, which is the government department for forestry in Great Britain. It serves as the forestry department of the Scottish Executive (the government of Scotland) by advising on and implementing forestry policy in Scotland. Its mission is to protect and expand Scotland's forests and woodlands and increase their value to society and the environment.

Forestry Commission Scotland manages 660,000 hectares of national forests and other land to provide a wide range of benefits, including timber production, public recreation, nature conservation, environmental protection and rural development. It also supports other forest and woodland owners by providing grants to plant, regenerate, manage and improve woodlands, licences to fell trees, and advice and regulation.

It is directed by Scottish Ministers through a Great Britain Board of Commissioners and a National Committee for Scotland, and funded by the Scottish Parliament. It works closely with the Scottish Executive, particularly the Environment and Rural Affairs Department, to deliver the Scottish Forestry Strategy, which is closely integrated with other aspects of rural land use and rural economic policy. It also contributes to many aspects of wider Scottish Executive policy such as the environment, health, education, rural transport and tourism.

For further information visit: www.forestry.gov.uk/scotland

Or telephone: 0845 FORESTS (0845 367 3787); enquiries@forestry.gsi.gov.uk

Donald Rodger

Donald Rodger is an independent arboricultural consultant based in East Lothian. He provides specialist advice on the care and management of amenity trees to a broad range of public and private sector clients throughout Scotland. He has a particular interest in heritage trees and has spent many years researching and recording them. He is a Chartered Forester, a Chartered Biologist and a Fellow and Registered Consultant of the Arboricultural Association.

For further information visit: www.donaldrodger.co.uk

References

The Drumlanrig Sycamore (page 10)
1 6th Earl of Haddington: *Forest Trees; Some Directions about the Raising of Forest Trees*. c.1761. p21.

The Auld Yew Tree of Loudoun (page 17)
1 Hutchison R: *On the Old and Remarkable Yew Trees in Scotland in Transactions of the Royal Arboricultural Society*, 1891. p379.

The Kailzie Larch (page 22)
1 *Principle Excursions of the Innerleithen Alpine Club during the Years*. 1889 – 94.

The Great Yew of Ormiston (page 36)
1 Martine J: *Reminiscences and Notices of the Parishes of the County of Haddington*. 1890. p153.

The Whittinghame Yew (page 38)
1 Martine: p251.

The Newbattle Abbey Sycamore (page 41)
1 Mitchell A. *Alan Mitchell's Trees of Britain*. Harper Collins, 1996. p.184.

Dalkeith Park Oaks (page 42)
1 Rackham O: *Trees and Woodland in the British Landscape*. 1976. p142.

Stephenson's Yew (page 44)
1 *'To Minnie', A Childs Garden of Verses*, 1885.
2 *'The Manse'*, in *Memories and Portraits*, 1887.

The Clachan Oak (page 68)
1 Highland and Agricultural Society of Scotland: *Old and Remarkable Trees in Scotland*. 1867. p177.

The Great Yew at Broich (page 72)
1 Highland and Agricultural Society of Scotland. p227.
2 Hutchison. p403.

Inchmahome Veterans (page 74)
1 Hunter T: *Woods, Forests and Estates of Perthshire*. 1883. p311.

Robert the Bruce's Yew (page 79)
1 Danielewski J: *Loch Lomond in Old Picture Postcards*. 1987.

The Mightiest Conifer in Europe (page 80)
1 Evelyn J: *Silva: or a Discourse of Forest Trees, and the Propagation of Timber in his Majesty's Dominions*. Royal Society, 15 October 1662.
2 *Transactions of the Scottish Arboricultural Society*. Volume ix: p174.
3 Elwes H and Henry A: *The Trees of Great Britain and Ireland*. Edinburgh. 1906 – 13. p730.

The Ardkinglas Grand Fir (page 82)
1 Tree Register of the British Isles. 2002.

Lady Miller's Beech (page 88)
1 Snoddy T G: *'Tween Forth and Tay*. 1966.

King James VI Sycamore (page 94)
1 Hunter T. p103.

The Scone Douglas Fir (page 96)
1 Elwes H and Henry A: p831.

The King of the Forest (page 98)
1 Urquhart J D: *Historical Sketches of Scone*. 1883.

The Pepperwell Oak (page 100)
1 Hunter T. p125.

The Mother and Father Trees (page 101)
1 Mitchell A L and House S: *David Douglas: Explorer and Botanist*. 1999. p187.

The Monzie Larch (page 104)
1 Mitchell A: *Alan Mitchell's Trees of Britain*. 1996. p73.
2 Highland and Agricultural Society of Scotland. p70.

The Parent Larch (page 106)
1 *Account of the larch plantation on the estates of Atholl and Dunkeld. Executed by the late John, Duke of Atholl*. Perth, 1832.
2 Mitchell A. p73.

The Fortingall Yew (page 128)
1 *Philosophical Transcations of the Royal Society. Vol 59*, Dec 1769. p23.
2 Neil, Dr: *Edinburgh Philosophical Journal*, 1833.
3 Loudon J C: *Arboretum et Fruticetum Britannicum or The Trees and Shrubs of Britain*. London, 1854. p2079.

The Darnaway Oak (page 142)
1 Phillips M T T: *The History of the Ancient Oak Forest of Darnaway and its Timber*. Scottish Forestry 55(3), 2001. p159.
2 Anon: *The Royal Scottish Arboricultural Society 4th Annual Excursion*. 1881.